Revision for
ENGLISH
Key Stage 3
• *with answers* •

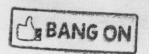

Revision for
ENGLISH
Key Stage 3
• *with answers* •

DIANA PRESS PAMELA McCAMLEY

JOHN MURRAY

© Diana Press and Pamela McCamley 1995

First published in 1995
by John Murray (Publishers) Ltd
50 Albemarle Street, London W1X 4BD

Reprinted 1996 (twice)

Cover design by John Townson/Creation
Layout by Fiona Webb
Typeset by Litho Link Ltd, Welshpool, Powys in 11/13pt Rockwell
Printed and Bound in Great Britain by St Edmundsbury Press, Bury St Edmunds

A CIP catalogue entry for this title can be obtained from the British Library

ISBN 0 7195 7025 5

■ CONTENTS

■ ACKNOWLEDGEMENTS

p. 10	The Mile by George Layton from a *Northern Childhood: The Fib and Other Stories* published by Longman Group UK Ltd
p. 11	From Boy by Roald Dahl published by Jonathan Cape Ltd and Penguin Books Ltd
p. 18	The Sea by James Reeves from *The Wandering Moon and Other Poems* , The James Reeves' Estate*
p. 19	Timothy Winters by Charles Causley from *Nine o'clock Bell* *
pp 24-26	From Home Sweet Home by Paul Groves and Nigel Grimshaw from *Six Plays for Today* published by John Murray
pp. 28 & 36	Sleeping Problems, September 1994 and Playing for your life, 10 March 1994 from the *Belfast Telegraph*
p. 29	Broken sofa yields its slice of history from *The Independent*, 26 November 1994
p. 37	From Three Lambs by Liam O'Flaherty from *The Short Stories of Liam O'Flaherty* published by Jonathan Cape Ltd
pp. 38 & 44	Mid-Term Break and The Early Purges by Seamus Heaney from *Death of a Naturalist* published by Faber and Faber Ltd
p. 39	Warning by Jenny Joseph from *Seven Themes in Modern Verse* published by Thomas Nelson & Sons Ltd
p. 41	From Shadows on the Lake by Catherine Sefton published by Hamish Hamilton
p. 42	From No Good Crying Now (author unknown)
p. 47	From Flower Express (Jersey) 1994
pp. 49-50	From The RSPB Catalogue (Spring/Summer 1994)
p. 51	Macleans Junior Mouth Guard; SmithKline Beecham Consumer Healthcare
p. 54	Illustration How the EU shapes up to vote from *The Times*, 9 June 1994, © Times Newspaper Limited, 1994

* While every effort has been made to trace copyright holders for the works reproduced in this book, the publishers apologise for any inadvertent omissions.

■ INTRODUCTION

The main purpose of this book is to provide students with a Key Stage 3 preparation framework. It may be used by students working independently, with the help of parents, or with teacher guidance.

In order to provide opportunities to develop skills and expertise, exercises ranging in levels of difficulty have been included. It is important that students learn from the exercises and tasks provided so that they can benefit and take account of their own strengths and weaknesses.

It is impossible to provide 'right and wrong' answers to tasks set for the English area of study. It must be stated at the outset that when 'answers', 'mark schemes' or 'guidelines' are provided they are only 'suggested answers'. Perhaps students might like to use the suggested answers as a second step in the process of drafting work. If the student completes a task, then studies the 'answer' provided, this might lead to a more effective final draft. Re-reading and drafting are vital stages in the developmental process in the study of English.

Speaking and Listening cannot be addressed in a book of this nature as this can only be successfully covered in the classroom under the guidance of the teacher. While Reading and Writing are the focus of this book, only a sample of work is presented. Equally, the language section covers only some of the many aspects of the English language. The book does not require the student to begin at the beginning and work through it until the concluding pages. Rather students should have the opportunity to work at areas which suit their individual needs.

Where space has been left below a question, students should use this for answer(s). Otherwise they will need to write their answer(s) on a separate sheet of paper.

We hope that you will enjoy working through this book and will find the exercises helpful and rewarding.

1 Language Exercises

■ FILLING IN A FORM

On many occasions you will find that you are asked to fill in a form. You may be applying for a job, a driving licence or a passport. As you are usually given only one form, it is important to fill it in neatly and carefully; an untidy form with mistakes scored out creates a very bad impression. If you are unsure about the correct spelling of a word, check it in a dictionary. It may be a good idea to fill in the form lightly in pencil; this can then be erased after completion in pen.

Remember to read instructions – if it states that the form or a particular section should be completed in block capitals then remember to do this.

If a section does not apply to you then a dash or the letters N/A (not applicable) are sufficient to show this. For practice, complete the Personal File which follows.

PERSONAL FILE

SURNAME (BLOCK CAPITALS) _____

FORENAME(S) _____

AGE (IN YEARS AND MONTHS) _____ **DATE OF BIRTH** _____

HEIGHT _____ cms **WEIGHT** _____ kg

COLOUR OF HAIR _____ **COLOUR OF EYES** _____

ADDRESS _____

_____ **POSTCODE** _____

SCHOOL _____

HOBBIES/INTERESTS _____

PETS _____

FAVOURITE POP GROUP/POP STAR _____

FAVOURITE TELEVISON PROGRAMMES _____

FAVOURITE MEAL _____

FAVOURITE BOOK _____ **AUTHOR** _____

NAMES AND AGES OF BROTHERS AND SISTERS _____

_____

NAMES OF PARENTS/GUARDIAN _____

_____

SIGNATURE _____ **DATE** _____

■ NOUNS AND ADJECTIVES

Nouns

A noun is often called a NAMING word. Common nouns name a class of persons, places, animals, things or qualities. Proper nouns name a particular person or place. For example:

boy, child – persons
town, village – places
rabbit, fish – animals
water, desk – things
beauty, happiness – qualities
Smith, London – name of particular person, place

Adjectives

Words which DESCRIBE nouns are called adjectives. Adjectives tell you more about the noun. For example:

the **blue** sky – blue (adj)
the **young** boy – young (adj)
the **stormy** sea – stormy (adj)

EXERCISE

List all the nouns and adjectives in these sentences and place them in the appropriate column below.

1. He was a kind, old man who lived in the dreary house.

2. The fast train sped along the twisting track.

3. Their school friends were thrilled to greet the new people in the neighbourhood.

4. The young boy walked nervously along the dark street.

5. The baby birds were preparing to leave the old tree.

6. My mother prepared some delicious sandwiches for our picnic.

7. The clever girl passed all the difficult exams.

8. The clear, blue sky was a welcome sight to the holiday-makers as they got off the plane in France.

9. As we walked along the dusty road we caught sight of the small, white cottage.

10. The excited children rushed to the park to play on the colourful swings.

Nouns	Adjectives
1. _____	1. _____
2. _____	2. _____
3. _____	3. _____
4. _____	4. _____
5. _____	5. _____
6. _____	6. _____
7. _____	7. _____
8. _____	8. _____
9. _____	9. _____
10. _____	10. _____

■ VERBS AND ADVERBS

A verb is an ACTION word, e.g.:

The team scored a goal, – **scored** (verb).

Sometimes verbs are made up of more than one word, e.g.:

He **was running**.

When you want to add some more information to the verb you use an ADVERB, e.g.:

He was running **quickly**.

Most adverbs end in -ly but some do not. For example:

He came **late**.   She worked **quietly there**.

EXERCISE

List all the verbs and adverbs in these sentences and place them in the appropriate column below.

1. The bored boy yawned lazily.

2. The train rumbled noisily through the station.

3. The teacher shouted angrily at the lazy pupil.

4. The old man snored loudly in his seat.

5. The water level in the river rose steadily.

6. We returned to the haunted castle very warily.

7. My father laughed happily to himself as he thought of early childhood memories.

8. The woman worked busily on the computer.

9. The police eyed the man suspiciously as he answered their questions cautiously.

10. The captain of the football team encouraged his team enthusiastically.

Verbs	Adverbs
1.	1.
2.	2.
3.	3.
4.	4.
5.	5.
6.	6.
7.	7.
8.	8.
9.	9.
10.	10.

■ CAPITAL LETTERS

Capital letters must be used in the following circumstances.

1. To start a sentence.

2. For the names of people or their initials, e.g. Joe Bloggs; J.H. Bloggs.

3. For the names of days of the week and months of the year, e.g. Friday, August.

4. For the names of places and countries, e.g. Manchester, England, and adjectives formed from proper nouns, e.g. English Victorian.

5. For the initials of organisations, e.g. BBC, BT.

6. For the titles of books, plays, or films, e.g. *Going Solo*, *Macbeth*, *The Flintstones*.

7. At the beginning of direct speech, even though it might not be the beginning of a sentence, e.g. Mary said "See you later."

8. Usually at the beginning of each new line in a poem.

EXERCISE

Write out the following sentences, putting capital letters in the appropriate places.

1. it rained last tuesday when we went to the football match.

_____

2. we are going on holiday in june to spain.

_____

3. mary bell is starting our school in september.

_____

4. my mother always says that she would prefer bbc to itv.

_____

5. the river seine runs through paris.

_____

6. my favourite book is _the growing pains of adrian mole_ by sue townsend.

_____

7. the girl screamed in a loud voice, "help, get me out of here".

_____

8. my favourite time of the year is christmas.

_____

9. the bbc presented _middlemarch_ by george eliot on television during last winter.

_____

10. everyone hates mondays but loves fridays.

_____

■ FULL STOPS AND COMMAS

Full Stops

REMINDER   The full stop should be used in the following circumstances.

    1. At the end of a sentence unless a question mark or exclamation mark is used.

    2. After initials (this also includes reference to personal qualifications, for example B.A.).*

    3. To show that a word has been shortened, for example Reverend – Rev.*

* You should be aware that there is a trend not to use full points. It is a matter of personal choice.

Commas

REMINDER   **1.** A comma must not be used instead of a full stop.

    2. A comma is used to separate words and phrases (groups of words) in a sentence to make it easier to read and understand the meaning.

Rules

1. Commas are used to separate items in a list except for the last two items which are joined by 'and', 'or' etc. For example:

The boy said that he studied English, French, German, Georgraphy and History.

2. Commas are used to mark off a phrase or group of words which tell you more about the main subject of the sentence. For example:

The old woman, who was rather poor and lived in a tumble-down house, had led a very lonely life.

3. Commas are used to separate phrases in a list. For example:

The girl rushed into the house, ran into the kitchen, ate her dinner quickly and then got changed to go out.

4. A comma is used when an adverb begins the sentence. For example:

Sadly, I returned to school after the holidays.

EXERCISE

Write out the following sentences, putting full stops and commas in the appropriate places.

1. He ran all the way to the bus stop but the bus pulled away just as he arrived

_____

2. Prof Knox was the expert on World War I

_____

3. Mary lived at 41 Appletree Road

_____

4. My favourite author is PP Barnes

_____

5. The star of the show is a tall girl with long dark hair

_____

6. The pop star who was visiting the nearby town is my favourite singer

_____

7. I hate spinach sprouts turnips and beetroot

_____

8. Happily the boy received his new birthday present

_____

9. The teacher stormed into the classroom threw down the books marched down through the rows of desks and demanded that the student should stand up

_____

_____

10. Frequently I go to the village which is a pretty little place to buy groceries such as butter milk tea and sugar

_____

_____

■ SENTENCES

1. A sentence must make sense. It is a complete unit on its own and it contains a verb.
2. It must have a capital letter at the beginning.
3. It must have a full stop at the end unless it is a question or an exclamation.
4. It can be short, simple, long or complicated.

EXERCISE

Here are some sentences and some phrases. Add a full stop to each sentence and after this write the letter S. Leave each phrase without a mark.

1. My aunt likes playing tennis
2. Somewhere in the middle of the forest
3. The pop star sang for two hours at the concert
4. The wind blowing in her hair
5. Everyone is welcome
6. All students with long hair must tie it back for sports activities
7. He was knocked down by the fast driver
8. Speeding along the highway at 70 m.p.h.
9. Overlooking the sea
10. The footballer was cheered by the supporters when he scored a goal

---

■ PARAGRAPHS

A paragraph is a group of sentences dealing with one central idea. There are very good reasons to write in paragraphs.

1. If writing was presented one line after another it would be very difficult for the eye to follow. Paragraphs help to make it easier to read and understand.
2. A new paragraph tells you one of the following:
   - something new is about to be introduced
   - some time has passed
   - there is a change of scene/setting
   - a new person is going to be introduced
   - there is a change of speaker in a conversation.

TASK 1

There are three paragraphs in the following extract. Where do you think each paragraph should begin?

Michael was looking forward to his holiday in Spain. He was going to spend three weeks in Benidorm staying in a villa which belonged to a friend. He grew very excited as he had not been to Spain before. The day of departure finally came. Michael arrived at the airport with plenty of time to spare. Take off was at 3 p.m. so he hurried to the foreign ticket desk. The plane left on time and the journey passed quickly. On arrival in Spain his friend was there to meet him. A short car ride took them to their villa and the holiday could begin.

TASK 2

If you learn to write in paragraphs it means that your work will be more carefully planned and properly organised.

Read the following description and see if you can decide why the writer has chosen to use three paragraphs.

MRS WALTON

She was a small, shrivelled up woman with a long pointed nose. When she moved from place to place she shuffled and stumbled, showing awkwardness and pain in every step. Her eyes were sunken and had long since lost any trace of youth or vitality. The clothes on her body seemed almost part of her, blending with her colourless form.

Mrs Walton lived in a small corner house which seemed to deny access to any visitors. It was dark and gloomy as indeed was the garden. Many times people in the neighbourhood had tried to help Mrs Walton by offering to do her shopping or tidy the garden but the only reply they received was a rebuke or a mutter that she didn't want to be "any trouble". No one seemed to visit her; she rarely received any mail. Could she have been as friendless throughout all her life?

I found it difficult to understand that someone could live such an isolated life. It was the existence of a hermit rather than the life of a lonely person because she seemed to have chosen her lifestyle. I frequently wondered what went on in her mind, how did she pass the time, and what past experiences had made her the mystery that she is today.

Paragraph 1 – a clear physical description of the central character is given. An artist could draw a picture of the woman from the words and phrases used to describe her.

Paragraph 2 – Mrs Walton's personality is presented here. We see that she is very reserved and rather mysterious.

Paragraph 3 – the author's thoughts and opinions are given here. We realise that the author is troubled and perplexed by this character.

QUESTION

Write a description of a person or a place, using the format set out above. Think carefully about the organisation of your work.

■ CONVERSATION

Words can sound different depending upon the way they are spoken. For example:

The simple question "What are you doing?" can be presented as an ordinary demand but if it is spoken in an angry tone it will have a totally different meaning.

When writing down conversation it is essential to follow certain rules as well as to convey the way the words are spoken. Read this conversation and then examine closely the rules which follow it.

Angrily she cried, "I hate the way the times of television programmes are changed just because of political broadcasts!"

He could not quite understand why she was so annoyed. "Well, I'm sorry", he said, "but I don't understand why it upsets you."

"I don't like watching my favourite soap later in the evening," she explained. "I like to eat dinner and then settle down to watch the TV while I am digesting my food." She paused and glanced at him. "Do you not understand that?"

He looked at her, and laughed. "Really, you are very conventional," he exclaimed. "For someone who likes to think she is so different you are really quite ordinary."

To his surprise she stormed away in a huff.

▬▬▬▬▬▬▬▬▬▬▬▬▬▬▬▬▬▬▬

1. All words which are actually spoken by any person must be inside speech marks (" ").
2. Start a new line every time there is a change of speaker.
3. Always begin the words which are spoken and start a new sentence with a capital letter.
4. Remember to close the speech marks before any interruption and open them again afterwards.
5. The words before a speech are always separated from it by a punctuation mark which is usually a comma but could also be a full stop.
6. The words which follow a speech are separated from it by a punctuation mark. This can be a comma, a question mark, an exclamation mark or a full stop.
7. If there is a break in the words being spoken within a single sentence, use commas to separate the two groups of words; then use a small letter to continue the speech.

Make up your own conversations following the format studied. Here are some suggestions.

1. Between a mother and daughter/son about homework.
2. Between a parent and child about the local disco.
3. Between two people about a football match.
4. Between two people about a pop concert.

EXERCISE 1

Here is an extract from a novel by George Layton which shows a conversation between a mother and her son about the school report he had just received. Write it out putting in the appropriate speech marks and punctuation marks.

THE MILE

Im sorry Mum . . .
She picked up the report again and started reading it for the fourth time
Its no good reading it again Mum Its not going to get any better
She slammed the report back on to the table
Dont you make cheeky remarks to me Im not in the mood for it
I hadnt meant it to be cheeky but I suppose it came out like that
I wouldnt say anything if I was you after reading this report
I shrugged my shoulders
Theres nothing much I can say is there
You can tell me what went wrong You told me you worked hard this term
I had told her Id worked hard but I hadnt
I did work hard Mum
Not according to this
She waved the report under my nose
Youre supposed to be taking your O Levels* next year What do you think is going to happen then
I shrugged my shoulders again and stared at my gammon and chips
I dont know

---

*GCSE replaced O Levels in 1988

EXERCISE 2

The extract on page 11 is from *Boy* by Roald Dahl. The owner of the sweetshop, Mrs Pratchett, is a very mean women who seems to dislike the boys so they decide to play a trick on her. Read the piece and then write it out, putting in speech marks and punctuation marks where appropriate.

BOY

Thus everything was arranged We were strutting a little as we entered the shop
We were the victors now and Mrs Pratchett was the victim She stood behind the counter and her small malignant pig-eyes watched us suspiciously as we came forward
One Sherbert Sucker please Thwaites said to her holding out his penny
I kept to the rear of the group and when I saw Mrs Pratchett turn her head away for a couple of seconds to fish a Sherbet Sucker out of the box I lifted the heavy glass lid of the Gobstopper jar and dropped the mouse in Then I replaced the lid as silently as possible My heart was thumping like mad and my hands had gone all sweaty
And one Bootlace please I heard Thwaites saying When I turned round I saw Mrs Pratchett holding out the Bootlace in her filthy fingers
I dont want all the lot of you troopin in ere if only one of you is buyin she screamed at us Now beat it Go on get out
As soon as we were outside we broke into a run Did you do it they shouted at me
Of course I did I said
Well done you they cried What a super show
I felt like a hero I *was* a hero It was marvellous to be so popular

---

■ APOSTROPHE (1) OWNERSHIP

The apostrophe is always placed after the owner or the owners as shown in the examples below.

The cats tail swung from side to side.
Who owned the tail?
The cat.
Place the apostrophe after the cat.
The cat's tail swung from side to side.

The boys books were in their schoolbags.
Who owned the books?
The boys
Place the apostrophe after the boys.
The boys' books were in their schoolbags.

The childrens presents were in their stockings.
Who owned the presents?
The children
Place the apostrophe after the children.
The children's presents were in their stockings.

EXERCISE

Now place the missing apostrophes in the following sentences.

1. Catherines coat was found in the playground.

   _____

2. The football teams new strip goes on sale today.

   _____

▶

---

3. The thieves stole the workmans tools.

_____

4. The thieves stole the workmens tools.

_____

5. Lack of exercise is putting peoples health at risk.

_____

6. The teachers meeting was held in the library.

_____

7. The workers canteen serves delicious meals.

_____

8. The farm workers disturbed a wasps nest.

_____

9. We stayed three days on our grandfathers farm.

_____

10. Mr Smiths new car is parked in his driveway.

_____

■ APOSTROPHE (2) CONTRACTION

Sometimes a word is shortened or two words are combined to form one word. When this happens an apostrophe is used to show that a letter or letters have been left out. Contractions are used chiefly in conversation when it is usual to speak more quickly.

Some commonly used contractions are:

isn't	in place of	is not	– the apostrophe replaces the missing letter o.
we're	in place of	we are	– the apostrophe replaces the missing letter a.
it's	in place of	it is	– the apostrophe replaces the missing letter i.

EXERCISE

Each of the following sentences contains two words from which a contracted word can be formed. Write out these two words and beside them write their shortened form. For example, did not = didn't

1. He does not enjoy playing football.

_____

2. It is going to snow tonight.

_____
▶

3. There will be chocolate cake for dessert.

_____

4. The boys could not reach the bird's nest.

_____

5. Who would like to go to the seaside today?

_____

6. I might not be able to go with you to the school disco.

_____

7. I am sure I locked the garage door before I left.

_____

8. They are coming to visit us next week.

_____

9. We had a delicious meal in the new restaurant.

_____

10. What is the time?

_____

■ CONFUSING WORDS

Some words can be very confusing because even though they sound similar they have completely different meanings. It is very important to use these words correctly. Here are two which must not be confused:

where/were
there/their

Where indicates place.
Where is the book?
[The question asks in which place the book is situated.]

Were is the verb or action word.
They **were** running to catch a bus.
[**were** is part of the verb which shows what the subjects are doing.]

Their shows that something belongs to people.
They put on **their** shoes.
[the shoes belong to "they"]

In all other instances **there** is used. For example:

to indicate place	She ran over **there**.
to mean 'in that matter'	I do not agree with you **there**.
to emphasise or call attention	Hey you, **there**!
in impersonal forms like there is, there are etc.	**There** were many people on the bus.
to exclaim satisfaction or dismay	**There**! What did I tell you!

EXERCISE

Fill in the blank spaces.

1. _____ [There/Their] is plenty to eat in the kitchen.

2. They _____ [where/were] rushing to get to school before assembly started.

3. The man wanted to know _____ [where/were] the hospital was.

4. The girls _____ [where/were] told by _____ [there/their] mother to tidy _____ [there/their] room.

5. _____ [Where/Were] _____ [where/were] they going on holiday?

N.B. You should really be able to distinguish between **where** and **were** because they should be pronounced differently.

■ HOMOPHONES

Words which are pronounced alike are called homophones. For example:

there;	their; they're
two;	too; to
son;	sun
no;	know
write;	right
would	wood
none;	nun
piece;	peace

Can you think of any others?
    Write five sentences each containing two homophones. For example:
    Make sure you **write** down the **right** answer.

■ ABBREVIATION

You will often see capital letter abbreviations used in many different places. Each of the letters stands for a word. Frequently used words and phrases are written in a shortened form to save time, for example GCSE.

EXERCISE 1

What do the following initials stand for? Remember, abbreviations in general use are explained in most good dictionaries.

1. O.H.M.S. on a letter.

_____

2. P.T.O. at the bottom of a page.

_____

3. M.P. after a person's name.

_____

4. C.O.D. on a sales docket.

_____

5. R.S.V.P. at the bottom of an invitation.

_____

▶

6. V.W. on the bonnet of a car.

_____

7. R.I.P. on a gravestone.

_____

8. A.D. after a date.

_____

9. A.W.O.L. on a soldier's report.

_____

10. H.R.H. before a member of the royal family's name.

_____

EXERCISE 2

Write each of the following words in full.

1. Dr. _____

2. St. _____

3. Sat. _____

4. Dept. _____

5. max. _____

6. Rev. _____

7. cm. _____

8. Sen. _____

9. Sq. _____

10. min. _____

11. etc. _____

12. p.s. _____

13. e.g. _____

14. i.e. _____

15. N.B. _____

EXERCISE 3

Write this advertisement without using abbreviations

Flat to Let
S.c. apt. n'r St. Mary's Hosp. Slps 4.
L'nge, ftd kitchen, 2 dbl b'rms, bthrm.
C.H. Ph. Sml gdn. £150 pm.
Tel. 284691 btwn 6–9pm

_____

_____

_____

_____

_____

■ WORDS FROM OTHER LANGUAGES

Many words from other languages have entered the English language and are in common use today.

EXERCISE 1

Match each word (now considered part of everyday English) with its correct meaning. Number 1 has been done for you. You may wish to use a dictionary to look up meanings.

1. dungarees (Indian)	A	recording on tape	**1N**
2. chalet (Swiss)	B	a killer	
3. idiot (Greek)	C	cocoa flavoured substance	
4. lynch (American)	D	spying	
5. mousse (French)	E	made from sour milk	
6. biro (Hungarian)	F	an exact copy	
7. pasta (Italian)	G	to annoy	
8. mosquito (Spanish)	H	seizure of means of transport	
9. espresso (Italian)	I	an alcoholic beverage	
10. ski (Norwegian)	J	a frothy creamy substance	
11. creche (French)	K	to do something alone	
12. sauna (Finnish)	L	moving quickly over snow	
13. kindergarten (German)	M	a stupid person	
14. algebra (Arabic)	N	trousers made of thick strong cloth	
15. bungalow (Indian)	O	a place where babies/young children are looked after	
16. yoghurt (Turkish)	P	tomato sauce	
17. ketchup (Chinese)	Q	a dried paste made from flour and cut into shapes	
18. assassin (Arabic)	R	a fly which bites	
19. chocolate (Red Indian)	S	a ball point pen	
20. hijack (American)	T	somewhere to shelter from the snow	
21. video (Latin)	U	a quick cup of coffee	
22. photograph (Greek)	V	a house with only one storey	
23. lager (German)	W	hot and steamy place	
24. espionage (French)	X	school for little children	
25. hassle (American)	Y	using letters instead of numbers	
26. solo (Italian)	Z	to execute someone without a proper trial.	

EXERCISE 2

From which languages do these words come? A dictionary should be used for this task.

1. bandit _____

2. species _____

3. phenomenon _____

4. memorandum _____

5. dilettante _____

6. cherub _____

■ METAPHOR AND ONOMATOPOEIA

The poem on page 18, *The Sea* by James Reeves, presents the reader with a picture of the sea. The poet creates this picture by using words and comparisons in much the same way that an artist uses colour and texture.

In order to appreciate this poem fully you must understand what the following words mean: METAPHOR and ONOMATOPOEIA.

Metaphor

A metaphor is a comparison between two things without the use of the words 'like', 'as' or 'than'. It is when you want to really emphasise the description by saying that something is the object mentioned without actually meaning it literally. The description is emphasised by saying that something is something else without it being literally true. For example, in the poem *My Sister Jane* by Ted Hughes the speaker gives a very uncomplimentary picture of his sister:

'My sister's nothing but a great big crow.'

The main point that the speaker is trying to make is that his sister looks and behaves like a crow without actually meaning that she is one.

Onomatopoeia

As well as adding description to a word picture a poet or writer can add sound too. The poet often wants us to hear what is happening as well as see what is happening. To do this he/she uses onomatopoeia. This is when the sound of the word reflects the meaning of the word. For example:

the tick tock of the clock
the screech of the car tyres
the tinkle of the bell

With such words you can actually hear the sound of the object being described.

It is important to be able to identify a metaphor and refer to onomatopoeia and to explain what effect they have on a piece of writing.

TASK

Now read *The Sea* by James Reeves. Read the poem three times: first, to understand what the poem is about; second, to consider the language of the poem; third, to decide your personal response to it.

THE SEA

The sea is a hungry dog
Giant and grey.
He rolls on the beach all day.
With his clashing teeth and shaggy jaws,
Hour upon hour he gnaws
The rumbling, tumbling stones,
And 'Bones, bones, bones, bones!'
The giant sea-dog moans.
Licking his greasy paws.

And when the night wind roars
And the moon rocks in the stormy cloud,
He bounds to his feet and snuffs and sniffs
Shaking his wet sides over the cliffs,
And howls and hollos long and loud.

But on quiet days in May or June,
When even the grasses on the dune
Play no more their reedy tune,
With his head between his paws
He lies on the sandy shores,
So quiet, so quiet, he scarcely snores.

QUESTIONS

1. What is the comparison being made in this poem?   (3 marks)

2. Pick out three adjectives which describe the dog. Why are these words good descriptions of the sea?   (6 marks)

3. In each verse we see the sea in different ways. Can you explain these three ways?   (15 marks)

4. The sound of the sea is very clear in this poem. Pick out six onomatopoeic words and say why they are appropriate.   (10 marks)

5. Do you like this poem? Give your own thoughts about the poem explaining why you think the word pictures created are effective.   (6 marks)

(Total 40 marks)

■ METAPHORS, ONOMATOPOEIA AND SIMILES

Read the following poem by Charles Causley and then attempt the tasks which follow.

TIMOTHY WINTERS

Timothy Winters comes to school
With eyes as wide as a football-pool,
Ears like bombs and teeth like splinters;
A blitz of a boy is Timothy Winters.

His belly is white, his neck is dark,
And his hair is an exclamation mark;
His clothes are enough to scare a crow,
And through his britches the blue winds blow.

When teacher talks he won't hear a word,
And he shoots down dead the arithmetic bird;
He licks the patterns off his plate,
And he's not even heard of the Welfare State.

Timothy Winters has bloody feet,
And he lives in a house on Suez Street;
He sleeps in a sack on the kitchen floor,
And they say there aren't boys like him any more.

Old Man Winters likes his beer,
And his missus ran off with a bombardier;
Grandma sits in the grate with a gin,
And Timothy's dosed with an aspirin.

The Welfare Worker lies awake,
But the law's as tricky as a ten-foot snake;
So Timothy Winters drinks his cup,
And slowly goes on growing up.

At Morning Prayers the Master helves,
For children less fortunate than ourselves;
And the loudest response in the room is when,
Timothy Winters roars 'Amen!'

So come one angel, come on ten:
Timothy Winters says 'Amen
Amen amen amen amen.'
Timothy Winters, Lord.

     Amen

A **simile** states a likeness between two things which are different in other ways. A simile usually begins with 'like' or 'as'. For example:

He cut through the log like a knife through butter.
She is as fit as a fiddle.

For example, in verse 1 Timothy's teeth are described as being 'like splinters'. Why do you think the poet has used this comparison and what picture is he trying to create in your mind? This type of comparison is a simile.

TASK 1
Work through the poem and make a list of the other similes used and explain the picture the poet is trying to create.

In verse 1 Timothy is said to be 'a blitz of a boy'. Blitz was a word used to describe wartime bombing raids.
   What mental picture of Timothy is the poet trying to create in your mind when he uses this image? This type of comparison is a metaphor (see page 17).

TASK 2
Now work through the poem and make a list of the other metaphors used. Explain the effect of each.

TASK 3
Describe Timothy's appearance. How does the poet create the impression that Timothy is not being cared for?

TASK 4
Give details of Timothy's family background and say why you think the Welfare Worker lies awake at night.

TASK 5
Explain the meaning of the last two verses.

N.B. helves means prays.

TASK 6
Read the following and show whether each is a simile or a metaphor.

1. Her eyes shone like diamonds. _____

2. The moon's a balloon. _____

3. Silver-hatted mushrooms. _____

4. The car flew down the road. _____

5. She's as pretty as a picture. _____

6. They were as quiet as mice. _____

7. It was raining cats and dogs. _____

8. The boy ran like the wind. _____

9. Her teeth were like pearls. _____

10. The gardener has green fingers. _____

2 Types of Writing

■ WRITING A STORY

Everyone likes to listen to stories. We tell stories to one another everyday without realising it, for example we explain what happened on the way to school or at school. When we tell stories we are showing that information has been gathered, and that observation of details concerning setting and people has taken place. We are always watching and listening to what happens in the world around us.

   If we are always telling stories, then writing a story shouldn't be difficult. It will be necessary to think carefully about the subject of the story and to plan how ideas can be most effectively presented. Let us look at the stages we go through before we write a story.

1. Write down the title of the story, if one has been given.
2. Brainstorm, i.e. write down everything that comes into your mind about the subject, placing the title in the middle of the page.

Example

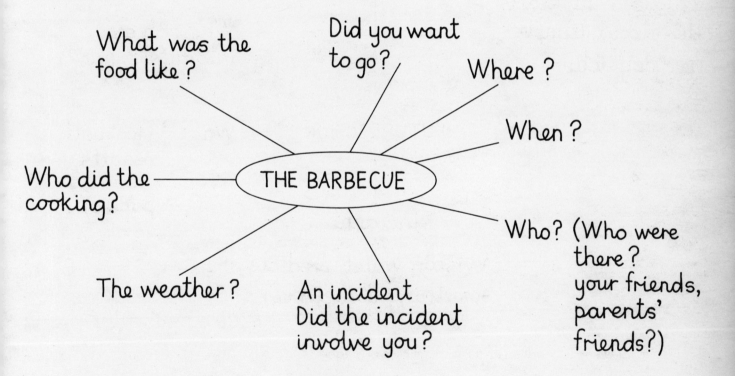

3. Once the ideas have been sorted out, it should be easy to decide which area to concentrate on, for example an incident or the development of the characters.
4. There must be an effective introduction – remember the first few lines will either encourage a reader to read on or make them decide not to bother. The setting, the situation and the character or characters must be interesting and intrigue a reader so that they want to consider future developments.
5. If you have planned your ideas properly the middle should develop fairly easily. Present the story or plot, unfolding it stage by stage or show the central character or characters moving towards a goal.
6. The ending is crucial too. A new idea should never be introduced in the last stages of a story. Decide if the ending is going to be gentle or pleasant or if it will be dramatic. A short sentence or question can be an effective dramatic ending.

▬▬▬▬▬▬▬▬▬▬▬▬▬▬▬▬▬▬▬▬▬▬

7. Try to base the story on something already heard, seen or read. Very few people are truly original thinkers, for example Shakespeare based his plays on other people's stories and all writers base their writing on the ideas of others. Naturally they put their own interpretation on to the situation or character so that eventually the outcome bears little resemblance to the orginal work.

8. Always check over your work to ensure that spelling, punctuation, grammar and style are correct.

TASK 1
Write a story about someone who can see into the future.

Problems

(a) How to make this story realistic – too often this type of task ends with the writer saying ' . . then I woke up.'

(b) Who will the story involve? – someone I know because I can deal with character features more easily.

(c) The story doesn't have a title – give a broad one, e.g. *Future Vision*.

Brainstorm (write down everything which comes into your mind on the subject. Do not worry about order at this stage.)

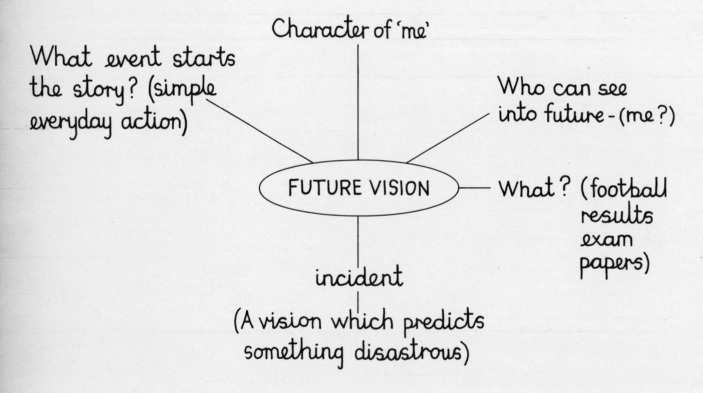

Here is a story which was written on this subject by a boy aged 14.

FUTURE VISION

NAME: John Smith
AGE: 14
ADDRESS: 40, Hightown Street, Newtown.
NO. OF YOYOS REQUIRED: 1

I filled in the application form for the 'Frosties Super Sparkling Yoyos' like this. The Frosties yoyos were silly little toys from which you were supposed to get hours of endless fun. But you actually got them, played with them for a few minutes and then threw them in a corner and didn't play with them for years. It is at this point that I should confess that I wasn't sending for them for me. It was my younger brother's Christmas present.

Christmas. Already? The one thing I have to do is exams. Chemistry today, but I wasn't sweating. I was so cool about the whole thing that when I got to the exam room, I started to revise History, instead of Chemistry. You see, I have an advantage. Two nights before, I dreamt of the exam paper, and all its questions. So when I received my paper, I knew all the questions, and had revised all the answers. It was a doddle.

Two years ago, I dreamt that my bike had been stolen. The next day I woke up and found that my bike was gone. Last year I had a dream about my team, Manchester United doing the double. The odds were 30–1, so I put £10 on them. Man. Utd. did do the double, so last May I collected £300 from my local bookie. He was not a happy man. So all in all, my 'future vision' is pretty good and reliable.

The day of my chemistry exam was Thursday. I went to bed that night, knowing that I had done well at chemistry. That night I had a terrible dream. It started with a calendar which read 9th December, that was this Sunday. Then I saw that the calendar was on a secretary's desk. "Go to gate 9," she said to an elderly couple. Outside gate 9 was a plane. Standing beside the plane was a man who had one of the hatches open and was fiddling with the mechanics of the plane. As soon as people started boarding, the man ran away. The plane took off but soon crashed, because the fuel line had been cut.

I woke up in a cold sweat, and shouted. My mum came in to calm me down. I went into school that day but just couldn't concentrate on my 27 page geography exam. I could not be sure whether that was a vision or just a dream. After all, there is a difference between foreseeing a chemistry paper and foreseeing a major plane crash. The next night, Friday night, I went to bed and dreamt the same thing again, except at the end of the dream there was a picture of one of those war-type posters with a man pointing and he was saying "Your country needs you!"

I woke up on Saturday, knowing that this was a vision and something had to be done. At around eleven o'clock I picked up the phone and called the airport.

"Hello?" a guy on the other end said. I told him all that I knew and thought.

"So you, a 14-year-old boy, are trying to tell me to shut down all tomorrow's flights because you had a dream?" he said.

"That's right," I said, and even I knew how stupid it sounded.

"Get off the line, you stupid prank-caller. Next time you want to waste my time, make it more believable," he shouted and slammed down the phone.

I spent the rest of the day sitting in and playing computer games, whilst trying to think of a way to stop the plane from flying. At 10.30 p.m. it hit me. It was drastic, but it had to be done.

On Sunday I woke up early. I took one of my dad's hankies, and at 9.53 p.m. I picked up the phone, put the hanky on the receiver and started dialling. I deepened my voice and when someone answered, I said "Hello?"

"Yes?" came the reply. This was a different person from yesterday.

"I've left a bomb somewhere on your premises. It is set to detonate sometime today."

"You've done what?"

"You heard me!" I said and slammed down the phone quickly, because I didn't want to be traced. That's that then, I thought.

That night I watched the news, and heard:

"Newtown Airport was at a stand still after an anonymous caller told of a bomb at the airport. A bomb was found in a suitcase, and all planes were checked over, and every plane found to be intact. Other news . . .

That's strange, I thought. My dream must have been wrong, but I got it right. That's even better. I then went to bed, happy knowing that I had saved some lives. All in a day's work for – 'Future Vision Man!'

Although this is a very clever imaginative story it could have been improved by revising and redrafting.

1. The pupil should have checked over his writing to ensure that punctuation was correct. He used too many commas – Look for the sentence beginning 'Two nights before . . .'
2. Sentence length could have been more varied. He has a tendency to use a lot of short sentences.
3. More description could have been included to break up the mainly factual approach of the story.

TASK 2

Use these titles to practise writing stories. Remember to follow the guidelines set out above. If you can, discuss ideas for your story with someone else.

1. Alone in the House

2. Sunday Dinner

3. The Fire

4. The Quarrel

5. Write a story to illustrate the topic 'Curiosity Killed the Cat'

6. Begin a story with the words 'I wish I were . . .'

7. Family Life

8. Out of Work

9. The Collector

10. The Long Journey

■ EMPATHETIC WRITING (WRITING FROM ANOTHER'S POINT OF VIEW)

According to the writer Harper Lee in *To Kill a Mocking Bird*, 'You never really understand a person until you consider things from his point of view – until you climb into his skin and walk around in it'. This idea is very important in the study of English. Frequently we are asked to consider things from another person's point of view; to think about their thoughts and feelings on a particular situation.

In order to do this properly these guidelines should be followed:

• write in the first person ('I').

• give an account of the events as they occur.

• try to identify the feelings of the 'I' of the piece – the feelings might change as the passage/poem progresses.

• give plenty of detail.

TASK

Read *Mid-Term Break* on page 38. Imagine you are the boy in the poem. Explain your account of the day and describe your feelings about what happened. Write about 300–400 words.

■ SCRIPTS AND DIALOGUE

Read the following excerpt from a short play, from *Six Plays for Today* by Paul Groves and Nigel Grimshaw. Simon, Keith, Andrea, Louise and Louise's baby have squatted in an empty country cottage. They have been discovered and the police, accompanied by the owners of the cottage, Mr and Mrs Barker, have arrived to ask them to leave.

HOME SWEET HOME

(*Upstairs,* **Simon** *and* **Keith** *are standing near an open window*)

POLICEMAN: (*voice off*) Will whoever is in there come out and talk to me, please?
KEITH: Take no notice.
POLICEMAN: Will you please come out, all of you?

SIMON: What do you want?

POLICEMAN: I have a man here who claims to be the owner of this cottage. Will you tell me what right you have in there, sir?

SIMON: Squatters' rights.

MRS BARKER: (*voice off*) This is our home. It's our retirement home.

SIMON: We're not budging.

POLICEMAN: It would be best if you all came out quietly.

MR BARKER: You've no right to be there.

SIMON: I expect it's a second home for you. We've got no home.

MR BARKER: It's not. We're selling our house in the town to buy this one. We're going to retire here.

MRS BARKER: We're going to do this place up.

SIMON: So you can afford two houses. We can't afford one.

POLICEWOMAN: (*voice off*) It would help if you stopped shouting and came down here.

(**Andrea** *comes in*)

ANDREA: Where are we going to live? You tell me that.

POLICEWOMAN: Where did you come from?

ANDREA: You try two years in a leaking caravan.

POLICEMAN: I can get other officers.

ANDREA: Bullies. What a country!

(**Louise** *comes in*)

LOUISE: We have a sick baby in here.

MRS BARKER: What a way to treat pensioners. I shall faint. I know I will.

MR BARKER: There, dear. We've worked all our lives for a house in the country.

SIMON: We've worked too, when we've been able to find work, but we've got nothing.

ANDREA: You give us a decent home.

LOUISE: Then we'll come out all right, but not before.

KEITH: Yes, go and fetch someone on the Council.

MRS BARKER: Are they gypsies?

POLICEWOMAN: I don't think so.

POLICEWOMAN: (*voice off*) I'll give you one last chance to come out. I have an order to get you out.

SIMON: Stand by the door, Keith.

LOUISE: The baby's ill and in pain. It could be appendicitis. We'll have to take him to hospital.

SIMON: As soon as we open that door, they're in.

LOUISE: We've got no choice. He's been awake all night.

POLICEWOMAN: (*voice off*) Let us in, please.

KEITH: Give him some more medicine.

LOUISE: It's no good, Keith.

ANDREA: We must think of the baby.

SIMON: Well, it was nice while it lasted. Take off the planks, Keith.

(**Keith** *starts to do this*)

LOUISE: We'll never have that swing you dreamt of.

ANDREA: No picnics under the apple tree.

LOUISE: Goodbye garden.

ANDREA: Goodbye house.

(*The four squatters leave the house*)

(*Some minutes later.* **Mr and Mrs Barker** *enter cautiously*)

MRS BARKER: Have they done any damage?

MR BARKER: I'll have to have a good look.

MRS BARKER: What a state it's in. I'm sure they're gypsies. Can we sue them?

MR BARKER: I'll have to look into it.

MRS BARKER: What a way to treat pensioners.

MR BARKER: I don't know what this country's coming to. To think that I fought in the war so people could have a decent life.

MRS BARKER: Some people seem to think they can have things for nothing. Forty years I worked in that biscuit factory.

MR BARKER: Let's get the camping stove going and have a cup of tea.

MRS BARKER: I thought the country would suit my nerves better. What a start. I'm all of a tremble.

MR BARKER: I'll make you a nice cup of tea, love.

TASK 1

Follow the format used in the extract for setting out the words spoken by each character. Remember to include any stage directions.

The squatters and the owners of the cottage are interviewed **separately** the next day by a television reporter.

1. Write a play scene in which the squatters answer the reporter's questions.

2. Write a play scene in which the owners answer the reporter's questions.
   Remember to check your spelling, punctuation, etc.

Try to make each scene about a page long, approximately 250 words.

This is an extract from *The Taming of the Shrew* by William Shakespeare. The play concerns a young girl, Katharina, who is very hot-tempered and determined. Her father wants her to get married so that he will not have the responsibility of looking after her any longer. He also has another daughter, Bianca, whom he prefers but because she is the younger daughter she cannot get married until her sister is married. Petruchio, a good-humoured and high-spirited gentleman, agrees that he will marry Katharina provided he is given a suitable dowry (money) by her father. Katharina is used to being rough with her sister and getting her own way so when she meets Petruchio she is amazed and shocked.

This extract takes place just after the marriage of Petruchio and Katharina. It is an account given by Signior Gremio. Read it carefully.

TAMING OF THE SHREW

Enter Gremio

TRANIO: Signior Gremio, came you from the church?	
GREMIO: As willingly as *e'er* I came from school.	ever
TRANIO: And is the bride and bridegroom coming home?	
GREMIO: A bridegroom, say you? *'tis* a groom indeed,	it is
A grumbling groom, and that the girl shall find.	
TRANIO: Curster than she? why, 'tis impossible.	
GREMIO: Why, he's a devil, a devil, a very fiend.	
TRANIO: Why, she's a devil, a devil, the devil's *dam*.	mother
GREMIO: Tut! she's a lamb, a dove, a fool to him.	
I'll tell you, Sir Lucentio; When the priest	
Should ask – if Katharine should be his wife,	
"Ay, by gogs-wouns," quoth he; and swore so loud	
That, all amaz'd, the priest let fall the book:	
And, as he stoop'd again to take it up.	
This mad-brain'd bridegroom took him such a cuff,	
That down fell priest and book, and book and priest;	
"Now take them up," quoth he, "if any list."	

Tranio: What said the wench, when he arose again?	
Gremio: Trembled and shook; for why, he stamp'd, and swore,	
As if the vicar meant to *cozen* him.	defraud, cheat
But after many ceremonies done,	
He calls for wine! – "A health," quoth he, as if	
He had been aboard, *carousing* to his mates	having a noisy party
After a storm: – *Quaff'd* off the muscadel,	drank some wine
And threw the *sops* all in the *sexton's* face;	remains church warden
Having no other reason, –	
But that his beard grew thin and *hungerly*,	wispy
And seem'd to ask him sops as he was drinking.	
This done, he took the bride about the neck,	
And kiss'd her lips with such a clamorous smack,	
That, at the parting, all the church did echo.	
And I, seeing this, came thence for very shame;	
And after me, I know, the *rout* is coming:	assembled company of revellers
Such a mad marriage never was before.	
Hark, hark! I hear the minstrels play.	

TASK 2

Write an account of the wedding in your own words as if you were a reporter for a newspaper. As you read make notes on the main happenings. Remember to use an appropriate headline and try to describe how this was a wedding with a difference. (Refer to instructions for writing a newspaper article on page 29).

■ LETTERS (BUSINESS OR FORMAL)

Points to remember

It is important to set out a letter properly. Remember that the reader of your letter will judge you according to the way you set out your letter as well as the content of your letter. This is how you should set out a business letter. (There is a trend not to use any punctuation in an address. It is a matter of personal choice.)

```
                                          72 Brock Street,
                                          Bangor,
                                          BG 72 8PS.
                                          4 March 1995
```

```
The Editor,
The World Newspaper,
Bangor,
BG72 7GS.

Dear Sir/Madam,
```

_____

_____

_____

_____

_____

_____

_____

```
                         Yours faithfully,
```

_____

Note the following points

1. Both addresses are presented with each line directly underneath the one above it.
2. All words in the address are written in full.
3. There is an imaginary margin around the page.
4. When the letter is addressed 'Dear Sir/Madam . . .' it should be signed 'Yours faithfully'. When the letter is addressed to the recipient by name, for example 'Dear Mr Jones . . .' it should be signed 'Yours sincerely'.
5. The reason for writing the letter is stated clearly at the beginning.
6. There is a suitable conclusion at the end of your letter.
7. In a formal letter the tone should always be polite.

TASK

The following letter was included in the letters column of a local newspaper. Write a reply to the letter including the following points.

1. A member of your family has a sleep problem.

2. You want to help him/her.

3. You would like an information pack.

The tone of the letter should be polite and formal. Remember once you have written your letter you should check for any mistakes you might have made in punctuation, spelling, grammar and style.

Sleeping problems

DO you, one of your family, or someone you know have sleep problems?

Many people experience sleep problems, varying from difficulty in getting to sleep, through constantly moving or waking, nightmares and night terrors to hardly sleeping at all.

So what causes it and what can be done; should you change your diet, routine, job, or lifestyle. Perhaps get more exercise or less, eat or have a drink just before you go to bed or not, play music, do relaxation exercises or count sheep. Surprisingly no one knows. This causes many drugs to be prescribed, maybe covering up the problem for a while.

Sleep problems are rarely considered directly life threatening, yet they are a major cause of accidents, large and small, causing injury, financial loss and deaths, as well as many divorces, and reducing the quality of life for many people.

Up to now many people, even those directly affected, have not recognised it as a serious problem. I hope I can persuade you, that together we can solve these problems for the majority of people.

If this is important to you, then please write enclosing two stamps for an information pack. This explains the little that is known and how we hope to work together establishing a support group, sharing knowledge, experiences, and trying out the numerous potential cures.

Working together, through the support group, we expect to solve at least 80pc of sleep problems. Where it is a medical problem, we hope to give you the information and confidence to ask for treatment.

Keith Park

UK Sleep Support Group,
450 Aberdare Enterprise Centre,
Aberaman Industrial Park,
Mid Glamorgan CF44 6DA.

Belfast Telegraph, September 1994

■ LETTERS (FORMAL)

Check that you know the layout of a business letter – see page 28.

TASK

Refer to the advertisement 'Make Mother's Day' on page 47.

Imagine that you ordered some flowers from a company such as 'Flower Express' and that they arrived late and were not fresh. Write a letter of complaint to an imaginary company asking for a refund. Make up a name and address. Remember to make your point strongly but politely.

Think about:

a) Layout

b) Content

c) Tone and vocabulary

■ NEWSPAPER ARTICLE

If you are writing an article for a newspaper it is important to follow certain guidelines.

1. The headline should catch the reader's attention.
2. Most good headlines give the main point of the story.
3. Humour or puns are sometimes used to catch the eye.
4. Some headlines emphasise the sound of words to create a dramatic effect by using **alliteration** (where the first letter is repeated at the beginning of several words, (e.g. Football Fans Flee.)
5. Some headlines are very exaggerated but it is better not to mislead your reader.
6. Paragraphs are used to break up the main body of the article.
7. The main facts of the story should be revealed in the first few paragraphs, answering the what, why, when, who and where of the story.
8. Sometimes an article is broken up by pictures with captions to explain these pictures.

No. 5   Nos. 1 and 2   No. 3

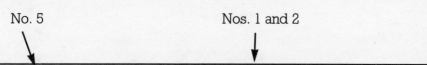

Broken sofa yields its slice of history

Possibly the world's oldest corned beef sandwich has been discovered inside a sofa in Peterborough, Cambridgeshire.

The 69-year-old sandwich, with a bite taken out of one side, was found together with a page from the *War Cry*, a shoe shop catalogue and a lunch-time shopping list for two corned beef sandwiches.

The 1920s snack was found by 87-year-old Harry Landin while breaking up his old sofa after his family and friends had turned down his offer to give it to them. Mr Landin said the sandwich was so cunningly hidden it could only be found when the sofa was taken apart.

Mr Landin said he thought the workman who built the sofa had probably eaten one sandwich, hastily taken a bite from the other and then thrown it, together with the rubbish, inside the sofa before finishing his job. "In those days you had to eat as you went along – there were no 10-minute breaks," he said.

He took the sandwich to Peterborough Museum, where the assistant curator, Elizabeth Davies, pronounced it inedible. She said: "The filling looks like corned beef, but my guess is it's really cheese.

"I've never seen anything like it before. The closest I've come to it is some dessicated rats which were about 300 years old," she added.

Ms Davies said there was no definitive way of dating the sandwich because radio carbon dating is not accurate over such a short timescale.

Mr Landin said that he was considering possible uses for the sandwich. "I think I'll just put it in the shed and forget about it. It's not much use to anyone, is it?"

But he is thinking of entering it for next year's Turner Prize. He said: "I suppose I'd have as good a chance as anybody, but I don't know where the art would come in.

"But someone also said they wouldn't be surprised if British Rail was caught trying to sell it," he added.

Danny Penman

Independent, 26 November 1994

No. 7   No. 6

Here are some newspaper headlines all based on the subject of noise pollution.

Torture of the neighbour forced to listen to Whitney Houston

Complaints about noise disturbance are on the rise

AIRCRAFT NOISE MADE ME ILL

GHETTO BLASTER USED TO DROWN OUT BUDGIES

Here are some facts and figures about noise and the effects of noise.
1. One in three people said their home life was spoilt by noise from traffic, neighbours, aircraft and trains.
2. Over 84,000 people made a formal complaint about noise between 1991–92, according to The Institute of Environmental Health Officers (IEHO).
3. Frequent disturbance by noise such as loud music can cause physical symptoms, for example headaches, stomach pain and depression.
4. Many complaints about noise are more to do with taste than volume – the neighbours' choice of music offends rather than the volume it is being played at.
5. These are the ten most common noise complaints: noisy neighbours, construction sites, factories/pubs/shops/offices/restaurants, burglar/car alarms, noisy parties, road works, barking dogs, traffic, radio playing in the street, aircraft.

TASK
Carefully study the information above and then write an article for your local newspaper on the subject of noise. Write about 200 words.

■ DISCURSIVE ESSAY

In this type of essay it is necessary to consider all the different points of view about a given topic. Titles may range from discussing the pros and cons of school uniform or the advantages and disadvantages of homework to the rights and wrongs of capital or corporal punishment.

What you, the writer, must do, however, is consider BOTH SIDES of the question objectively and then in your conclusion you may state your own viewpoint.

Planning is of the utmost importance and in this section the stages of planning a discursive essay entitled 'Television is a bad influence on young people today' will be worked through.

Stage 1 – The introduction

Begin by introducing the topic. You may consider its history, any recent controversies or simply give relevant background information to place your discussion in context. In the case of television you may wish to consider some of the following points, all of which have increased our exposure to the influence of television:

- there has been an increase in the number of channels
- programmes are now being broadcast 24 hours a day
- many homes now have more than one television set
- many young people now have a television in their bedroom
- development of video
- introduction of satellite services.

Stage 2 – The pros and cons

The second stage is to look at the pros and cons of your topic. No matter what your personal feelings, you must consider both sides of the argument. It is particularly useful when writing this type of essay to take a page and brainstorm your ideas – that is jot down all your thoughts as they come into your mind.

In this way you are less likely to leave out important points. Next organise your ideas. Make two lists – for and against. Some of the ideas you may wish to consider for this essay are listed below.

Points in favour:
* young people are encouraged to stay at home
* they have a wide variety of top class programmes to choose from
* it's 'free' entertainment
* there are programmes specifically for young people
* young people may learn from educational/schools programmes
* international sports events can be watched by everyone.

Points against:
* young people become 'couch potatoes'
* they may be exposed to violence and bad language.
* there can be a lack of parental control over what young people watch
* young people may be discouraged from developing other interests
* school work and reading may suffer.

Try to add at least five more points to each box.

Your points should then be organised into two well written, clearly explained paragraphs.

Stage 3 – Conclusions

In the concluding paragraph of your essay you should weigh up the arguments you have made and explain your own thoughts on the topic. It is possible that you will not agree or disagree completely with the statement you have been discussing. You may agree (or disagree) but only up to a point and this is perfectly acceptable. Explain your own opinions honestly and clearly and do not hesitate to make suggestions of your own, but be careful not to have unrealistic expectations, for example television companies are highly unlikely to cut down on their broadcasting time.

TASK

Using the plan and guidance provided, now write the discursive essay – 'Television is a bad influence on young people today'.

Write discursive essays on the following topics.

1. Experiments on animals should be banned. Discuss.
2. The school holidays are too long. Discuss.
3. Capital punishment should be reintroduced for violent crimes. Discuss.
4. Smoking should be banned in public places. Discuss.

■ REDRAFTING

Read the following conversation between a customer and the manager of a shoe shop.

MAKING A COMPLAINT

MANAGER:	Yes? What do you want?
CUSTOMER:	Are you the bloke that's in charge?
MANAGER:	I'm the person in charge of the ladies' shoe department.
CUSTOMER:	Well, what are you going to do about these shoes?
MANAGER:	What's wrong with them?
CUSTOMER:	Are you blind? The heel has come off them. I can't wear them any more.
MANAGER:	What's that got to do with me?

CUSTOMER:	I bought them in this stupid shop, that's what.
MANAGER:	Can you prove that?
CUSTOMER:	Yeah, I bought them from some blonde girl last week.
MANAGER:	That's hardly proof of purchase.
CUSTOMER:	Why don't you ask her then?
MANAGER:	Who?
CUSTOMER:	That blonde girl, who do you think?
MANAGER:	I have lots of blonde girls working for me, many on a temporary basis.
CUSTOMER:	Well, find her and ask her.
MANAGER:	My staff can't be expected to remember every person they sell a pair of shoes to. Anyway a receipt is the only acceptable proof of purchase.
CUSTOMER:	Well, I haven't got one.
MANAGER:	In that case I can't help you at all. Good morning.
CUSTOMER:	You'll not catch me in this stupid shop again!

TASK

Rewrite the above conversation. This time, however, the customer makes her complaint politely and the manager is more helpful. She manages to convince the manager to replace the unsatisfactory shoes.

■ WRITING A BOOK REVIEW (1) FICTION

When writing a review of a novel you have read it is important to organise your account so that you do not simply write a summary of the story and a description of the characters, but convey a sense of your appreciation of the book as a whole.

Introductory paragraph

It is best to keep the introductory paragraph of your book review brief. You should begin by stating the full title of the book and the name of its author. You may, if you wish, include details of the publisher, the book's publication history and its current price. Any biographical information about the author may also be mentioned at this point.

Second paragraph

In the second paragraph you should give a brief outline of the story. It is important not to try to recall every detail but instead to write a summary of the plot in your own words. Describe the way in which the story develops, mentioning key events. You may wish to describe a favourite incident in some detail – if you do this, explain why you particularly enjoyed this part of the book.

Third paragraph

Paragraph three should contain studies of the main characters. You should consider their part in the novel and the importance of their contribution to the plot. Think about their personalities and discuss any changes which take place as the novel progresses. Try to decide whether the characters are true to life, and if the author has succeeded in creating convincing people.

Fourth paragraph

In the fourth paragraph you should look at the way the book is written and also at any issues or themes that the author may be trying to highlight.

Listed below are some questions you might ask.

- What type of book is it?
  For example romance, adventure, a school story, fantasy.
- Who is the intended audience? Is the book aimed at a children's or teenage market or could it be read and enjoyed by adults too?

- Is it suitable for both boys and girls?
- Is the author trying to do more than write a straightforward story? Are any themes discussed? For example, loneliness, family life, prejudice, bullying, friendship, injustice.
- Is the story fast-moving and exciting? Are there unexpected twists in the story or can you tell what is going to happen next?
- Does the book contain long passages of description or is it mainly dialogue?
- Is the story easy to follow?
- Is the setting of the book clearly described?
- Could you identify/sympathise with the characters?

N.B. These questions are only intended as guidance to help you focus your thoughts and you should, of course, feel free to add any ideas or comments of your own.

Final paragraph

In the final paragraph of your review you should give your personal opinion of the book. Did you enjoy it? Try to give your reasons. Would you recommend it to others of your own age? If possible state where the book can be bought or borrowed.

TASK
Review a book you have read recently, using the guidelines given above.

■ WRITING A BOOK REVIEW (2) NON-FICTION

It is possible that you will also be asked to write a review of a non-fiction book. You can use the basic novel review plan by making a few minor changes.

The format of your introduction remains the same, but paragraph two should outline the contents of your book rather than retelling the story. In paragraph three you should consider the layout and format of your non-fiction book.

Some other points to consider:
- are the contents clearly indicated?
- has the book a detailed index?
- is there a good balance of pictures to text (and vice versa)?
- has colour been used to enhance pictures and diagrams?
- is the book attractive and clearly set out?

In paragraph four you should look at the way the book is written and try to judge its usefulness as an information or text book.

Some points to consider:
- as far as you can tell are the contents accurate and up to date?
- are they clearly explained and easy to understand?
- who is the intended audience? Is the book aimed at a children's or teenage market or at an adult readership?

The format of your final paragraph remains the same as for a fiction book review.

TASK
Write a review of a non-fiction book you have read recently, using the guidelines above.

■ REPORT WRITING

Reports vary from the glossy and expensive reports issued by large companies or government departments, to the simple typed or hand-written report compiled by someone in the course of his or her daily work.

However, the basic layout, the headings and the type of information included are essentially the same in any report.

Making a report involves:

- stating its purpose (i.e. why it is being written)
- finding out information about the subject-matter
- presenting it in a logical order under different headings
- including visual material (graphs, diagrams, statistics, photographs, etc.) where appropriate
- reaching conclusions
- making recommendations.

Suggested layout and sub headings

1. **Title**

   Your title should be clearly stated and it may also be necessary to indicate who the report is for. For example 'A report on . . . for the consideration of . . .'

2. **Terms of reference**

   In this section you should give relevant background information explaining why the report is being written and what its purpose is.

3. **Procedure**

   Include here a description of how you went about finding your information, for example reference material used, details of any interviews and questionnaires, also any other research methods used.

4. **Findings**

   Present your facts or evidence in an ordered logical sequence. Include only what is relevant to the topic, keep your language simple and direct, and always bear in mind the audience you are writing for.
   At this stage you may wish to include any visual material which may clarify or reinforce the points you are making, such as graphs, diagrams, photographs.

5. **Conclusions**

   Summarise (briefly and clearly) what you have found in this part of your report. Your conclusions should follow on logically and naturally from the facts and evidence you have presented in the previous section.

6. **Recommendations**

   These are your practical proposals for change and/or improvement based on what you have stated in your report.

7. Your signature and the date conclude your report.

TITLE
A Report on the facilities of your school library and how they could be improved.

TERMS OF REFERENCE
This report is being written for the Board of Governors and the librarian of Newtown Comprehensive College. Its purpose is to investigate the usage of the library by different form groups and how this can be encouraged and increased.

PROCEDURE
The school librarian was interviewed. Members of different form classes were asked to fill in the questionnaire and their responses collated. Other school libraries were also visited.

FINDINGS
The school librarian stated that the library was busiest during breaktimes and lunchtimes, particularly on rainy days. It was also used by teachers and their classes for project and research activities. Pupils reported that they enjoyed the opportunities to browse, but their favourite authors were not well represented. They felt many of the books were old-fashioned and unattractive. The library was cold, unwelcoming and the seats were uncomfortable. All of the magazines were of an academic nature. The pupils expressed a desire to use the

▶

---

library after school hours. Visits to other libraries revealed a warm, welcoming atmosphere with colourful book and magazine displays. Some of these libraries provided the opportunity to borrow audio and video cassettes.

CONCLUSIONS
The library of Newtown Comprehensive College would benefit from re-stocking with up-to-date literature and non-fiction books. The room could be made more attractive and comfortable and its services extended.

RECOMMENDATIONS
1. Existing stock should be evaluated and new books should be purchased.
2. The room should be re-decorated and new furniture bought.
3. Displays should be given a high priority.
4. The possibility of using the library as a Homework Centre after school should be investigated.
5. The library should become a focus for activities such as story-telling and debates.
6. A pupil committee should be set up to advise on the purchase of new stock.

A.J. Smith
27.11.94

TASK
Write a report:

1. For *Radio Times*, who are doing a survey of typical family viewing based on the number of hours and the types of television programmes watched by three members of your family over the period of a weekend.
2. For your local councillor, who is campaigning for additional funding on the facilities offered by your local leisure centre/local library/youth club.

■ EFFECTIVE NOTE TAKING

It is important to develop the skill of effective note taking in the early years of secondary school. It is impossible to remember everything you read or hear so to be able to take a set of well-organised notes which make sense when read later is of immense value to any student.

Note taking may be needed when:
- planning an essay
- revising for exams
- reading for information
- preparation for giving a talk
- when a topic is being explained in class.

How to take notes
This is a skill which comes with practice and there are no hard-and-fast rules about note taking. It will soon become obvious, however, which notes are useful to you and which are not (sometimes it may help to look at a friend's notes).

Some ideas are as follows.
1. Do not try to write down everything. Listen carefully and try to condense what has been said in your own words.
2. If making notes from a book, skim read the relevant section first in order to make sense of the whole piece. Make sure you understand what you have read before attempting to summarise the rest.
3. Do not write in sentences – key words or phrases are enough to trigger your memory when reading the notes later.
4. When you have finished, read over your notes – if you can't make sense of them now it is unlikely that you will later.
5. Check that you have included all the important points and/or ideas.
6. Emphasise any key points or ideas by underlining them.

If you follow these steps you should develop a personal style of note taking and build up a skill which will stand you in good stead, not only in English, but in all your other subjects as well.

TASK
Read the following passage and make notes on the key points.

Playing for your life

By Claire McGahan

KIDS of the '90s are more likely to run into coronary heart problems later in life than their parents or grandparents ever were according to a local physical exercise expert.

Hot on the heels of national calls for tough action to correct serious deficiencies in children's diets, Dr Colin Boreham, Queen's University PE department, has warned that if children continue to follow the sedentary lifestyle that has become the norm, they could be tomorrow's heart disease victims.

Dr Colin Boreham said that kids of the '90s do not exercise enough, particularly in Northern Ireland where more than 47pc of primary schools have no gymnasium; there is one of the highest levels of car ownership, and the lowest percentage – just 10pc of children who walk or cycle to school.

"This inactivity is putting our children's health in jeopardy and increasing their risk of heart disease, obesity and other health problems at a much earlier age," says Dr Boreham.

A number of factors can be attributed to this less active lifestyle of the younger generation. Much blame has been placed on the phenomenal growth in popularity of video and computer games, and television viewing.

A further contributory factor is the growing reluctance of parents to give children the freedom to play unsupervised.

Street games, exploring in the park and walking to the local shop have become activities of the past in today's urban environment.

"In the past, it was felt that children were more like free range hens – able to run around and do as they pleased outdoors.

"Now, understandably and for obvious reasons, parents have to watch over their children much more. For example, the majority of children are taken to school, instead of being allowed to cycle."

Dr Boreham believes that this lack of 'play-time' deprives children of a natural, unstructured exercise and learning through self-discovery. He is an active supporter of children's adventure playgrounds, where children can enjoy vigorous play under supervision.

The question for parents now is how else to stimulate the kids to get into the habit of taking exercise. An adventure playground where they can go as a family is the ideal way for kids to realise exercise is every bit as much fun as watching TV or playing a video game."

One such adventure playground is the indoor Gulliver's Kingdom, in Boucher Crescent, Belfast. Up to 250 children at any one time can run and play to their hearts content with a dazzling array of ropes, swings and slides.

Says manager Brid Rice: "We think this is ideal for kids to use up a lot of energy. Parents can bring all the family and be sure they are safe and well supervised at all times."

Belfast Telegraph, 10 March 1994

3 Response to Reading

Read the following extract very carefully at least three times: first, to understand what the passage is about; secondly, to consider the detail of the story; thirdly, to decide upon your personal response to it.

The extract is the opening of the short story *Three Lambs* by Liam O'Flaherty. It describes a boy's excitement as he prepares to witness the birth of some lambs.

THREE LAMBS

Little Michael rose before dawn. He tried to make as little noise as possible. He ate two slices of bread and butter and drank a cup of milk, athough he hated cold milk with bread and butter in the morning. But on an occasion like this, what did it matter what a boy ate? He was going out to watch the black sheep having a lamb. His father had mentioned the night before that the black sheep was sure to lamb that morning, and of course there was a prize, three pancakes, for the first one who saw the lamb.

He lifted the latch gently and stole out. It was best not to let his brother John know he was going. He would be sure to want to come too. As he ran down the lane, his sleeves, brushing against the evergreen bushes, were wetted by the dew, and the tip of his cap was just visible above the hedge, bobbing up and down as he ran. He was in too great a hurry to open the gate and tore a little hole in the breast of his blue jersey climbing over it. But he didn't mind that. He would get another one on his thirteenth birthday.

He turned to the left from the main road, up a lane that led to the field where his father, the magistrate, kept his prize sheep. It was only a quarter of a mile, that lane, but he thought that it would never end and he kept tripping among the stones that strewed the road. It was so awkward to run on the stones wearing shoes, and it was too early in the year yet to be allowed to go barefooted. He envied Little Jimmy, the son of the farm labourer, who was allowed to go barefooted all the year round, even in the depths of winter, and who always had such wonderful cuts on his big toes, the envy of all the little boys in the village school.

He climbed over the fence leading into the fields, and, clapping his hands together, said "Oh, you devil," a swear word he had learned from Little Jimmy and of which he was very proud. He took off his shoes and stockings and hid them in a hole in the fence. Then he ran jumping, his bare heels looking like round brown spots as he tossed them up behind him. The grass was wet and the ground was hard, but he persuaded himself that it was great fun.

TASK

Answer these questions.

1. Why is Little Michael excited? (2 marks)

2. Write down five phrases in the passage which suggest that Little Michael is excited. (10 marks)

3. Describe the differences between Little Michael and Little Jimmy. (8 marks)

4. What do you think happens next? Describe Little Michael's thoughts and feelings as he witnesses the birth of a lamb. (20 marks)

You should include in your answer:

- an indication of Little Michael's mood (5 marks)

- the type of journey he has (5 marks)

- some idea of what happens when he finds the sheep. (10 marks)

(Total 50 marks)

■ POETRY

When given a poem to study it is essential to read it several times in order to make sure that you fully understand it.

Read the poem *Mid-Term Break* by Seamus Heaney three times: first, to understand what it is about; secondly, to consider the poet's use of language; thirdly, to decide upon your personal response to it as a poem.

MID-TERM BREAK

I sat all morning in the college sick bay
Counting bells knelling classes to a close.
At two o'clock our neighbours drove me home.

In the porch I met my father crying –
He had always taken funerals in his stride –
And Big Jim Evans saying it was a hard blow.

The baby cooed and laughed and rocked the pram
When I came in, and I was embarrassed
By old men standing up to shake my hand

And tell me they were 'sorry for my trouble';
Whispers informed strangers I was the eldest,
Away at school, as my mother held my hand

In hers and coughed out angry tearless sighs.
At ten o'clock the ambulance arrived
With the corpse, stanched and bandaged by the nurses.

Next morning I went up into the room. Snowdrops
And candles soothed the bedside; I saw him
for the first time in six weeks. Paler now,

Wearing a poppy bruise on his left temple,
He lay in the four foot box as in his cot.
No gaudy scars, the bumper knocked him clear.

A four foot box, a foot for every year.

TASK 1

Answer the following questions. Always remember that your answers should be in complete sentences. You should try to include as much detail as possible, and in your own words unless otherwise indicated.

1. It is only at the end of the poem that the reader finds out exactly what has happened to the poet's younger brother. In your own words briefly describe what the poem is about.   (3 marks)

2. Discuss the poet's choice of title for the poem.   (3 marks)

3. What effect is achieved by the use of the word 'knelling' in line 2?   (4 marks)

4. Why did the boy find his father's reaction surprising?   (3 marks)

5. Who was the only person acting normally, and why?   (2 marks)

6. Why was the boy embarrassed?   (2 marks)

7. What two phrases are used by neighbours in the poem to express sympathy. Why do you think the poet chose them?   (3 marks)

▶

8. In what way were the mother's reactions different from those of the father? (3 marks)

9. 'Snowdrops and candles soothed the bedside.' What is the effect of this phrase? (4 marks)

10. What two impressions does the poet wish to convey when he uses the description 'poppy' bruise? (3 marks)

11. Comment on the effect of the last line. (6 marks)

12. Do you like this poem or not? Give reasons for your opinion. (4 marks)

(Total 40 marks)

The following poem by Jenny Joseph presents us with a very unusual picture of an old person. You might be surprised by some of the ideas in it. Think carefully about this picture and then decide if you like this presentation of an old person.

WARNING

When I am an old woman I shall wear purple
With a red hat which doesn't go, and doesn't suit me
And I shall spend my pension on brandy and summer gloves
And satin sandals, and say we've no money for butter.
I shall sit down on the pavement when I'm tired
And gobble up samples in shops and press alarm bells
And run my stick along public railings
And make up for the sobriety of my youth.
I shall go out in my slippers in the rain
And pick the flowers in other people's gardens
And learn to spit.

You can wear terrible shirts and grow more fat
And eat three pounds of sausages at a go
Or only bread and pickle for a week
And hoard pens and pencils and beermats and things in boxes.

But now we must have clothes that keep us dry
And pay our rent and not swear in the street
And set a good example for the children.
We will have friends to dinner and read the papers.
But maybe I ought to practise a little now?
So people who know me are not too shocked and surprised
When suddenly I am old and start to wear purple.

TASK 2

Now answer these questions.

1. The poet seems to be looking forward to when she is old. Why do you think that this is so? Try to think of three reasons. (6 marks)

2. Name ten things which the poet will do when she is old. (10 marks)

3. Why can the poet not do these things now? (1 mark)

4. Why is this poem titled *Warning*? (3 marks)

5. You have been asked to write a newspaper article about the lady in this poem. Think of an eye-catching title. Decide whether she is to be presented in a favourable or unfavourable way. Write about 200 words. (10 marks)

(Total 30 marks)

Read this extract from *As You Like It* by William Shakespeare. Try to picture in your mind the people he is describing.

SEVEN AGES OF MAN

All the world's a stage,	
And all the men and women merely players;	
They have their exits and their entrances,	
And one man in his time plays many parts,	
This acts being seven ages. At first the infant,	
Mewling and puking in the nurses' arms:	
And then the whining schoolboy, with his satchel	
And shining morning face, creeping like snail	
Unwillingly to school. And then the lover,	
Sighing like furnace, with a woeful ballad	
Made to his mistress' eyebrow. Then, a soldier,	
Full of strange oaths, and bearded like a *pard*,	leopard
Jealous in honour, sudden and quick in quarrel,	
Seeking the bubble reputation	
Even in the cannon's mouth. And then, the justice,	
In fair round belly, with good *capon* lined,	young chicken
With eyes severe and beard of formal cut,	
Full of wise *saws*, and modern instances,	sayings
And so he plays his part. The sixth age shifts	
Into the lean and slippered *pantaloon*,	foolish old man
With spectacles on nose, and pouch on side,	
His youthful hose well saved, a world too wide	
For his shrunk *shank*; and his big manly voice,	leg
Turning again toward childish treble, pipes	
And whistles in his sound. Last scene of all,	
That ends this strange eventful history,	
Is second childishness and mere *oblivion*;	nothingness
Sans teeth, *sans* eyes, *sans* taste, *sans* everything.	without

TASK 3

Now answer these questions.

1. List the seven ages of man and briefly describe each one in your own words. (14 marks)

2. Why is the world described as a stage? Which words extend this metaphor? (6 marks)

3. Pick out two similes from this extract. Write them down. Explain the comparisons. (10 marks)

4. In your own words describe the very old man as he is presented in this extract. (6 marks)

5. Choose *one* of the stages and write about 200–300 words, describing an incident which may happen to someone at this stage of their life. (14 marks)

(Total 50 marks)

■ CHARACTER ANALYSIS

Reading becomes more interesting when you pick up all the clues presented to you. When you have done this you form a picture in your mind based upon information provided in the words and descriptions.

Carefully read this extract from *Shadows on The Lake* which is placed at the very end of the novel. The 'I', of the piece is called Annie Orr who is thirteen years old. Her brother has been involved in helping Allie Sharry whose father was kidnapped.

SHADOWS ON THE LAKE

I told her what I thought of her, because I thought she ought to know, and nobody else was going to tell her.

"You should never have used our Baxter," I told her. "You had no right to get him to do a dangerous thing like that. He might have been killed."

So might I, I was thinking.

"There was nobody else I could trust like I'd trust Baxter," she said.

I was silent for a minute. Maybe she wasn't as bad as I'd been painting her. She really did like him, even if she didn't fancy him. And she'd trusted him, and believed in him, which was more than I had. She knew all along he was straight and honest, I was the one who called him a thief, when he wasn't.

"You could have done it yourself!" I said, still peeved at her.

She had her answer off pat. She couldn't do it because the police were watching her, and they were all over the place.

"You used him," I said. "You made sheeps' eyes at him and used him. You let on you fancied him."

"I did not," she said. "He's not my boyfriend, if that is what you're getting at, or likely to be. We just get on with each other, that's all."

"You know that," I said. "You know you'll go off and marry someone like your father, with hotels and bags of money. But does Baxter know it?"

"If he doesn't, I can't help it," she said.

"You used him," I said, repeating it so that she would get it into her head.

"Look," she said. "It was use Baxter, or have my daddy killed on me. What would you have done?"

"I don't know," I said.

"And I'll tell you why Baxter did what he did," she said. "I'll tell you what you ought to know for yourself, already. He did what he did because he's a good person, not because he was going to get anything out of it."

"I do know that," I said.

"It's time you learned to trust people," she said. There was a spot of crimson in her cheek. She was really angry. "I just wish I had someone like Baxter for a brother, that's all."

I was still thinking about it when she dropped me back at our house.

Peter had the meal made, and we sat and had it, and I looked at my dad. I would have done the same as Allie Sharry, if I had thought it was what was needed to save him. She was right! She probably loved old Miles the same way I love Dad. She wasn't mean or bad or trying to use anybody, she was just doing the best she could for the people she loved.

My dad got up.

"I'm going for a dander by the lake," he said.

Something went *snap* inside me.

"I'm going with you!" I said.

He blinked at me.

"Pete's coming too," I said. "Aren't you, Peter. We'll go round to Runey and see if you can spot your old pike!"

And we did.

It was fine.

It was just fine.

We were down by the lake with the sun winking on it and I watched the pair of them and it made me fed up with myself for all the months and months I'd spent not trusting them, or anybody else, as if the whole world was a conspiracy against me because my mother died.

If my dad didn't tell me, he must have had his reasons.

"Listen to me," I said. "We're starting a new regime in this family! We're going to get this place all wound up again, and no more moping about, and no more arguments and going our own ways. We're all going to look after each other, and then we'll be fine."

"Is that one of your orders?" Peter said.

"Hairy git!" I told him.

We walked on round the lake, in the sunlight. We had all been like shadows, going on doing the things we have to do, with nothing new allowed to grow between us. Everything had been bottled up.

"You know what?" my dad said.

"What?" I said.

"You're getting to be a grand girl," he said.

TASK 1

Answer these questions using your own words.

1. List eight things you have learned about Baxter and what others thought of him. (8 marks)

2. List all the things you have learned about Allie Sharry and what others thought of her. (8 marks)

3. What has Annie learned as a result of this experience? (6 marks)

4. Imagine you are Annie. Write your diary entry, about 150 words, for the day after this event. (Refer to advice on empathetic writing at page 24.) (18 marks)

(Total 40 marks)

Note: If you can answer these questions in detail you have a very good understanding of each of the characters.

TASK 2

Read the following passage carefully and then answer the questions which follow. Answers should be written in complete sentences, and in your own words unless otherwise indicated.

Reading time: ten minutes

Time for answering questions: thirty minutes

NO GOOD CRYING NOW

I recall that rainy Saturday when I was about eight. Mum and I had to take my china doll, Jean, to be mended at a little shop called the Dolls' Hospital, because my friend Jane had dropped her on the pavement and her head had smashed into a hundred pieces. I let out such a piercing scream that at first Mum thought I'd been knocked over, and when I saw her face as I held the broken doll in my arms, I wished I had been. I wished it was my head that was broken.

In a mad frenzy she ordered me, Jane and Ida, my other friend who was also crying, to search every square inch of the pavement outside our house until every fragment was found. Crying and crawling around on my knees, I picked up a handful here and there, and we placed the tiny jagged pieces on a tablecloth. Mum shouted at me that this was the last I'd ever see of Jean again. She threatened to put her in the dustbin and it would serve me right for allowing Jane to hold her. Hadn't she warned me time and time again not to take Jean out into the street? She was such a precious doll given to me by my father when I was still a toddler. I was supposed to play with her indoors and only upstairs in the front room where there was a carpet, so that if I should drop her she wouldn't break.

My friends scooted off to their houses for dinner, Mum tied together the four corners of the tablecloth, then slapped my legs so hard all the way up the stairs as I hugged Jean's headless body, that I still felt the sting and could see the imprints of her fingers for hours afterwards. We had waited ages in the pouring rain for a 63 bus to take us to Peckham before Mum decided we must walk there because the shop closed for dinner between one o'clock and two. "I reckon we're going on a fool's errand anyway," she kept saying as we walked over the bridge. "It looks to me as if it's broken beyond repair. Perhaps this will teach you a lesson in future. I don't say these things for nothing, you know. Jane makes sure she doesn't bring any of her dolls out to play. It's always yours she breaks, she sees to that. You are a silly little fool. And it's no good crying now, you should have thought of all this before."

In the small, dark shop various limbs hung from hooks attached to lengths of string across the low ceiling. On hearing the tinkling door bell these grisly arms and legs began to dance swaying independently as the little old man emerged from somewhere in the back and caught them with the top of his head. His abundant auburn hair might well have been a wig since there wasn't a trace of grey, yet the rest of him looked at least eighty.

He kept wigs of different colours, black, blond and auburn in deep drawers under the wooden counter; some of them were styled wavy like his, others were curly or straight. Inside smaller drawers, glass eyeballs rattled and rolled about as he tried his best to match them, but his own eyes didn't match, for one was blue, the other brown and they stared blankly without blinking for several moments, behind gold-framed spectacles that magnified his odd-looking eyes.

He shook his head when he saw Jean. "Oh dear! Oh dear!" His voice was high-pitched as though he had swallowed one of the doll's voice boxes. "That's a very special doll, that is. I only keep a stock of average heads. I don't think I've got one big enough to fit, but I'll have a look." Dolls' heads of different sizes, fair-skinned with rosy cheeks and dark-skinned, but all with strangely smiling faces waited on shelves all around the shop for their bodies to be fitted with limbs attached. He examined each likely head with Jean's body but kept shaking his auburn locks and tutting. "No good! No good! The trouble is your doll isn't like the dolls I usually have brought to the Hospital."

"Well," explained Mum, "she's not really a doll at all, you know, she used to model baby clothes in a shop window." I knew that Jean was no ordinary doll. She was real. She could talk, but only to me. She listened to every word I said, but only my words. She didn't like Mum and Gran when they were cross with me, in fact she didn't care for them at all. She thought they were both miserable and should have their heads boiled for making me cry. She only liked me and we had secrets that nobody else knew about only Jane, but I wasn't sure about Jane, now this terrible accident had happened.

"I was wondering," Mum continued, "whether there was any possibility of your putting it together again. I know it's a lot to ask but you're so clever. I've brought all the bits and pieces along, that is, as many as we could find." She delved down into her shopping bag and carefully placed the table cloth tied in a bundle on top of the counter.

The man stroked his long auburn beard that might well have been doll's hair or perhaps he used his beard for all the bald-headed dolls that were brought to him.

"Well," he shrilled, "that depends on how many bits there are and how many bits are missing. It is a very big head and it's made from special china. I've not come across one like this before."

"They should all be here," said Mum, untying the corners and helping to spread out all the pieces, triangles, squares and oblongs. "Like a jigsaw puzzle, isn't it? I wouldn't know where to start." "Oh dear! Oh dear! It'll be a long job fixing all these pieces and I'll have to use some very special glue." "I don't mind how much it costs." said Mum, looking at me ferociously. "You'll have to go without your sweets and comics and we'll cut out going to the pictures on Saturday afternoons." "I'll do my best," the man squeaked, sorting out the pieces and putting them into little piles, "but it'll never be the same, you'll always see the cracks."

---

1. What did the girl's mother think when she heard her screaming? (1 mark)

2. Why did they have to go to the Dolls' Hospital? (1 mark)

3. Write out four facts we learn about the doll. (4 marks)

4. Where was the Dolls' Hospital? (1 mark)

5. There were two signs to show that the girl's mother had slapped her hard. What were they? (1 mark)

6. The mother was angry for three reasons. What were they? (3 marks)

7. Name at least two things that were unusual about the old man in the shop. (2 marks)

8. Why did the old man think he would not be able to fix the doll's head? (2 marks)

9. Why was the doll so special to the girl? Write at least sixty words in your answer. (5 marks)

10. Imagine you are the girl in the story looking back on this incident. Describe what happened and how you felt about it. Write between 100 and 150 words (10 marks)

(Total 30 marks)

TASK 3

Read the following poem by Seamus Heaney carefully and then answer the questions which follow.

THE EARLY PURGES

I was six when I first saw kittens drown.
Dan Taggart pitched them, 'the scraggy wee shits'.
Into a bucket: a frail metal sound.

Soft paws scraping like mad. But their tiny din
Was soon soused. They were slung on the snout
Of the pump and the water pumped in.

'Sure isn't it better for them now?" Dan said.
Like wet gloves they bobbed and shone till he sluiced
Them out on the dunghill, glossy and dead.

Suddenly frightened, for days I sadly hung
Round the yard, watching the three sogged remains
Turn mealy and crisp as old summer dung

Until I forgot them. But the fear came back
When Dan trapped big rats, snared rabbits, shot crows
Or, with a sickening tug, pulled old hens' necks.

Still, living displaces false sentiments
And now, when shrill pups are prodded to drown,
I just shrug 'Bloody pups'. It makes sense.

'Prevention of cruelty' talk cuts ice in town
Where they consider death unnatural.
But on well-run farms pests have to be kept down.

1. Describe in detail in your own words what happened to the kittens. (3 marks)

2. Quote four phrases from the first two verses which show how frail and helpless the kittens were. (4 marks)

3. To what are the kittens compared as they floated in the bucket? Name the figure of speech used. (2 marks)

4. What was the young boy's first reaction to the drowning of the kittens and how did he behave? (2 marks)

5. In your own words, how and why did Dan Taggart kill animals? What do his actions reveal about his attitude to animals? (7 marks)

6. How does the poet's attitude towards the killing of animals change as he grows older? Answer in your own words, then quote from the poem to back up your answer. (3 marks)

7. How do townspeople react to the killing of animals and why does the poet disagree? (4 marks)

8. What is your reaction to this poem? In about a hundred words say what you liked or disliked about it. You should mention what the poem is about, the language used and your response to its theme. (5 marks)

(Total 30 marks)

TASK 4

Imagine a conversation between Dan Taggart and a townsperson who believes that Dan is guilty of cruelty to animals. (Refer to conversation rules in the Language section.)

You should write 100–150 words.

TASK 5

Charles Dickens was a nineteenth-century writer whose portraits of people are very detailed and memorable.

Read this extract from *Hard Times* by Charles Dickens and answer the questions which follow.

MR BOUNDERBY

He was a rich man: banker, merchant, manufacturer, and what not. A big, loud man, with a stare, and a metallic laugh. A man made out of a coarse material, which seemed to have been stretched to make so much of him. A man with a great puffed head and forehead, swelled veins in his temples, and such a strained skin to his face that it seemed to hold his eyes open, and lift his eyebrows up. A man with a pervading appearance on him of being inflated like a balloon, and ready to start. A man who could never sufficiently vaunt himself a self-made man. A man who was always proclaiming, through that brassy speaking-trumpet of a voice of his, his old ignorance and his old poverty. A man who was the Bully of humility.

1. Explain in your own words Mr Bounderby's occupations. (4 marks)

2. Look at the first sentence of the passage. Why does Dickens list Bounderby's occupations and then add the phrase 'and what not'? (3 marks)

3. What do you think is meant by 'A big, loud man, with a stare and a metallic laugh'? (5 marks)

4. Dickens describes him as being 'inflated like a balloon'. What does this suggest to you? (3 marks)

5. Why do you think he is always boasting about 'his old ignorance and his old poverty'? (3 marks)

6. Do you think that Dickens wants us to like Bounderby? Give four reasons for your answer. (7 marks)

(Total 25 marks)

■ ADVERTISEMENTS

TASK 1

**Study the advertisement on page 47 carefully and then answer the questions which follow.
Remember, all answers should be in complete sentences.**

1. What is being offered to the consumer? (2 marks)

2. At whom do you think this advertisement is being aimed? (3 marks)

3. How much is the cheapest bouquet? (1 mark)

4. What is the difference between the two bouquets at £11.99? (2 marks)

5. What is included in the price of each order? (3 marks)

6. How is each bouquet packaged? (1 mark)

7. What are the two methods by which you can place your order? (2 marks)

8. How can you pay for the flowers? (Give three alternatives.) (3 marks)

9. What is the closing date for the order? (1 mark)

10. What details must be given if you wish to place an additional order? (4 marks)

11. Do you have to pay extra for postage? Which word tells you this? (2 marks)

12. List six words and phrases in this advertisement which imply that this is an offer not to be missed. (6 marks)

(Total 30 marks)

Make Mother's Day

10 longstem and 5 spray carnations £11.99

18 long-stemmed carnations £11.99

ONLY £8.99 ONE DOZEN CARNATIONS

Send her one dozen, luxury, longstem carnations by 1st Class Post for only £8.99! Included in the price are fern, flower food, and a personal message from you. All presented in a sturdy designer gift box, delivered to her door from Jersey.

Should you want to send a larger bouquet, we have two other great value for money offers featuring our luxury carnations both at the incredibly low price of £11.99 inclusive. Either phone your credit card order or send by post but remember we must receive it by MARCH 4th LATEST. Should you require additional orders please give the details on a separate piece of paper.

ORDER FORM
Orders must be received for Mother's Day by 4th March 1994

COMPLETE IN BLOCK CAPITALS

Please send bouquet to:

Name and address _____

Choose from	Price	Quantity	Amount
12 long-stemmed carnations	£8.99		
10 longstem+5 spray carnations	£11.99		
18 long-stemmed carnations	£11.99		

☐ I enclose my cheque/postal order for £ _____ payable to Flower Express Jersey

☐ or debit my Access-Visa-Switch

card No _____

Expiry date _____

Signature _____

Send to Flower Express Jersey, Woodside Farms, Trinity, Jersey, Channel Islands, JE3 5DN

Although the flowers are sent by first class post the exact delivery date cannot be guaranteed. REF: IND

My name _____

My address _____

Message (max 12 words) _____

Flower
EXPRESS JERSEY

For credit card orders
☎ **FREEPHONE 0800 393934**

TASK 2

Look carefully at this extract from a brochure advertising and selling products from The Royal Society for the Protection of Birds. When you have studied this extract thoroughly answer these questions.

1. Where is Leighton Moss Reserve? (3 marks)

2. Explain what you do when making a telephone order. (5 marks)

3. What would you order if you wanted to encourage butterflies to come into your garden and how much would it cost? (4 marks)

4. How long should you allow for the delivery of an item? (2 marks)

5. Explain the meaning of the following words and phrases:

elusive	(2 marks)
durable	(2 marks)
denotes	(2 marks)
embossed motif	(4 marks)
perennials	(2 marks)

6. Imagine you have been given approximately £20 to spend on your garden. State what you would buy and explain your choice. (8 marks)

7. Would you support the RSPB's work? Explain the reasons why you would or would not support them. (6 marks)

(Total 40 marks)

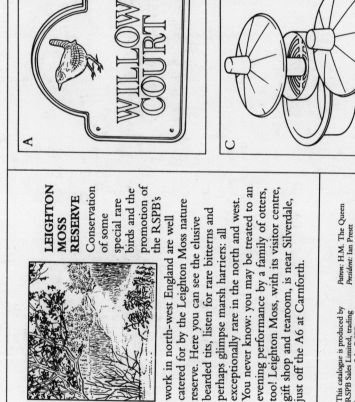

A WILLOW COURT

B 6 · RSPB EXCLUSIVE ·

C

D

E

F

LEIGHTON MOSS RESERVE

Conservation of some special rare birds and the promotion of the RSPB's work in north-west England are well catered for by the Leighton Moss nature reserve. Here you can see the elusive bearded tits, listen for rare bitterns and perhaps glimpse marsh harriers: all exceptionally rare in the north and west. You never know: you may be treated to an evening performance by a family of otters, too! Leighton Moss, with its visitor centre, gift shop and tearoom, is near Silverdale, just off the A6 at Carnforth.

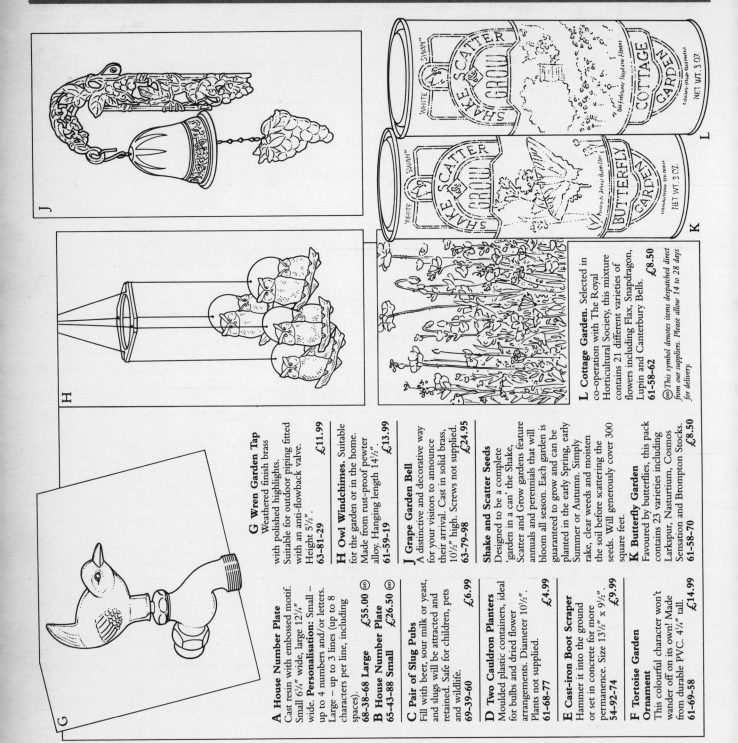

A House Number Plate
Cast resin with embossed motif. Small 6¼" wide, large 12¼" wide. **Personalisation:** Small – up to 4 numbers and/or letters. Large – up to 3 lines (up to 8 characters per line, including spaces).
68-38-68 Large   £55.00 ⊚
B House Number Plate
65-43-88 Small   £26.50 ⊚

C Pair of Slug Pubs
Fill with beer, sour milk or yeast, and slugs will be attracted and retained. Safe for children, pets and wildlife.
69-39-60   £6.99

D Two Cauldron Planters
Moulded plastic containers, ideal for bulbs and dried flower arrangements. Diameter 10½". Plants not supplied.
61-68-77   £4.99

E Cast-iron Boot Scraper
Hammer it into the ground or set in concrete for more permanence. Size 13½" x 9½".
54-92-74   £9.99

F Tortoise Garden Ornament
This colourful character won't wander off on its own! Made from durable PVC. 4¼" tall.
61-69-58   £14.99

G Wren Garden Tap
Weathered finish brass with polished highlights. Suitable for outdoor piping fitted with an anti-flowback valve. Height 5½".
63-81-29   £11.99

H Owl Windchimes. Suitable for the garden or in the home. Made from rust-proof pewter alloy. Hanging length 14½".
61-59-19   £13.99

J Grape Garden Bell
A distinctive and decorative way for your visitors to announce their arrival. Cast in solid brass, 10½" high. Screws not supplied.
63-79-98   £24.95

Shake and Scatter Seeds
Designed to be a complete 'garden in a can' the Shake, Scatter and Grow gardens feature annuals and perennials that will bloom all season. Each garden is guaranteed to grow and can be planted in the early Spring, early Summer or Autumn. Simply rake, clear weeds and moisten the soil before scattering the seeds. Will generously cover 300 square feet.

K Butterfly Garden
Favoured by butterflies, this pack contains 23 varieties including Larkspur, Nasturtium, Cosmos Sensation and Brompton Stocks.
61-58-70   £8.50

L Cottage Garden. Selected in co-operation with The Royal Horticultural Society, this mixture contains 21 different varieties of flowers including Flax, Snapdragon, Lupin and Canterbury Bells.
61-58-62   £8.50

⊚ This symbol denotes items despatched direct from our suppliers. Please allow 14 to 28 days for delivery.

■ ADVERTISING

The influence of advertising is increasing and it is important to be able to 'read between the lines' of an advertisement.

The questionnaire should help you to analyse any advertisement, not just this one.

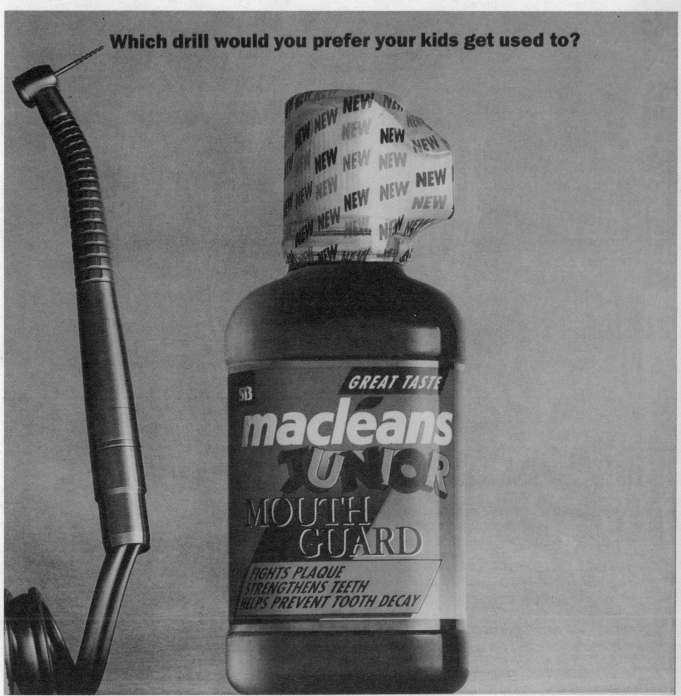

By the time they're twelve, 53% of children suffer from some form of tooth decay. And where tooth decay strikes, the drill soon follows.

That's something nobody relishes, least of all a dentist. So what exactly can you do to help?

Well, obviously make sure your kids have regular check-ups. And, of course, insist they brush after meals.

But you should also get them into the habit of using Macleans Junior Mouth Guard at least twice a day.

This is a mouthwash that has been specially formulated to provide young teeth with unbeatable protection. To that end, it contains a bacterial agent to attack plaque, plus fluoride to strengthen the teeth.

And because it's a liquid, it gets everywhere in the mouth, even those places a kid's toothbrush can't.

There's something else in our favour kids love its great taste. It's one drill they don't mind getting used to.

Macleans where a kid's toothbrush can't.

■ ADVERTISEMENT QUESTIONNAIRE

1. Q What is the product advertised?   Q What is the brand or make?

A _____   A _____

(2 marks)

2. Q What is it about the advertisement that first catches your attention and why?

A _____

_____

(1 mark)

3. Q Give a brief description of the layout of the advertisement.

A _____

_____

_____

(3 marks)

4. Q At what kind of customer is it aimed?

A _____

(1 mark)

5. Q How does it try to persuade those particular customers?

A _____

_____

(1 mark)

6. Q Does the advertisement play on any emotions, do you think? Which?

A _____

_____

(2 marks)

7. Q List some of the striking pictures/images and language it uses.

A Images	Language

(10 marks)

▶

8. Q What is there about the advertisement that is easy to remember?

A _____

_____

(3 marks)

9. Q Is there anything misleading about the advertisement and if so, what?

A _____

(1 mark)

10. Q What information does the advertisment NOT give that might otherwise help a customer make a better informed decision?

A _____

(1 mark)

11. Q What is YOUR opinion of the advertisement? Is it convincing? Would it persuade you to buy the product being advertised? Indicate your reasons.

A _____

_____

_____

_____

_____

_____

(5 marks)

(Total 30 marks)

■ OTHER WAYS OF PRESENTING INFORMATION

The European Union

HOW THE EU SHAPES UP TO VOTE

IRELAND
Population: 3.5m
Number of voters: 2.5m
Number of seats: 15
Date of vote: June 9
Main 1989 results:
Turnout: 68.3%
Fianna Fail: 6 seats
Fine Gael: 4 seats
Labour Party: 1 seat

ITALY
Population: 56.9m
Number of voters: 48.2m
Number of seats: 87 (81 in 1989)
Date of vote: June 12
Main 1989 results:
Turnout: 81%
Christian Democrats: 26 seats
Communists: 22 seats
Socialists: 12 seats

LUXEMBOURG
Population: 400,000
Number of voters: 212,740
Number of seats: 6
Date of vote: June 12
Main 1989 results:
Turnout: 87.4%
Christian Social Party: 3 seats
Socialists: 2 seats
Democratic Party: 1 seat

PORTUGAL
Population: 9.3m
Number of voters: 8.5m
Number of seats: 25 (24 in 1989)
Date of vote: June 12
Main 1989 results:
Turnout: 51.2%
Social Democrats: 9 seats
Socialists: 8 seats
Christian Democrats: 3 seats

SPAIN
Population: 39.5m
Number of voters: 31.6m
Number of seats: 64 (60 in 1989)
Date of vote: June 12
Main 1989 results:
Turnout: 54.6%
Socialists: 27 seats
Popular Party: 15 seats
United Left: 4 seats

GREECE
Population: 10.3m
Number of voters: 8.9m
Number of seats: 25 (24 in 1989)
Date of vote: June 12
Main 1989 results:
Turnout: 79.9%
Conservatives: 10 seats
Socialists: 9 seats
Left coalition: 4 seats

THE NETHERLANDS
Population: 15.4m
Number of voters: 11.7m
Number of seats: 31 (25 in 1989)
Date of vote: June 9
Main 1989 results:
Turnout: 47.2%
Christian Democrats: 10 seats
Labour Party: 8 seats
Right Liberals: 3 seats

GERMANY
Population: 81m
Number of voters: 60.2m
Number of seats: 99 (81 in 1989)
Date of vote: June 12
Main 1989 results:
Turnout: 62.3%
CDU/CSU: 32 seats
SPD: 31 seats
Greens: 8 seats
FDP: 4 seats

UK
Population: 58m
Number of voters: 43.7m
Number of seats: 87 (81 in 1989)
Date of vote: June 9
Main 1989 results:
Turnout: 36.2%
Labour Party: 45 seats
Conservative Party: 32 seats
Others: 4 seats

FRANCE
Population: 58m
Number of voters: 39m
Number of seats: 87 (81 in 1989)
Date of vote: June 12
Main 1989 results:
Turnout: 48.7%
UDF/RPR: 26 seats
Socialists: 22 seats
National Front: 10 seats

DENMARK
Population: 5.2m
Number of voters: 4m
Number of seats: 16
Date of vote: June 9
Main 1989 results:
Turnout: 46.2%
Social Democrats: 4 seats
Anti-EC Party: 4 seats
Liberals: 3 seats

BELGIUM
Population: 10m
Number of voters: 7.8m
Number of seats: 25 (24 in 1989)
Date of vote: June 12
Main 1989 results:
Turnout: 90.7%
Flemish CVP: 5 seats
Francophone PS: 5 seats
Flemish Socialists: 3 seats

Election facts
269 million votes can choose from more than 10,000 candidates on 300 lists across 12 countries. In 1989, there were 518 seats. Today there are 567 seats. 49 new seats have been added to accommodate a bigger German electorate following unification. Most new seats go to Germany but some also go to other EU member states.

1989 percentage share of seats in Euro-Parliament
38% Socialist Group
32% EPP Christian Democrat Group
30% Others

TASK

Using the map and the information given answer the following questions.

1. Name the three centres of the European Union. Say what is based in each centre. (6 marks)

2. Which countries in the European Union have the largest and smallest populations ? (2 marks)

3. How many MEPs were there altogether in 1994? (1 mark)

4. How many extra seats has Germany got since the 1989 election? Why? (2 marks)

5. Which country has 7.8 million voters? (1 mark)

6. Name the countries which have increased their number of seats since 1989. (9 marks)

7. Which political group had the highest percentage of seats in the 1989 Parliament? (1 mark)

8. What is surprising about the anti-EC party holding four of the Danish seats? (1 mark)

9. Write three paragraphs about the European Union.
   a) the countries, their size and electorate; b) the political parties;
   c) your opinion of European countries working together. (5 marks each)

10. Draw bar graphs to show:
    a) the number of seats each country had in 1989
    b) the number of seats each country had in 1994.
    What benefits can you see in presenting information in this way? (12 marks)

(Total 50 marks)

Ten teenage safety tips

Both teenage boys and girls can find themselves at risk, whether working at a part-time job or just out in the evening. So it is important for teenagers to try to follow these basic guidelines.

1. Always tell your parents where you are going and what time you intend to return.
2. Your parents should know how and where to contact you.
3. Try not to go out alone. If possible, make arrangements to go out with friends and return home with them.
4. If you do have to go out alone, arrange transport before you go to and from your destination – either with a friend or a relative or a taxi company. Someone responsible should know of your arrangements, and you should always make sure you have enough money with you.
5. Always have the correct change to make a telephone call or in an emergency don't hestitate to reverse the charges.
6. If your arranged transport fails to turn up and it seems as if you will be left alone, speak to someone responsible and ask to use a telephone to make alternative arrangements. Ask to stay with someone until transport arrives.

NEVER SET OFF ON YOUR OWN LATE AT NIGHT.

7. Don't accept a lift from someone you've just met or from a complete stranger.
8. Try to find part-time jobs such as babysitting on the recommendation of friends and be extremely careful about answering advertisements. It would be a good idea to go accompanied by a parent or a friend on the first day.
9. If, when you are working on a paper round, strangers invite you into their homes politely refuse and move on quickly.
10. Know how to make an emergency telephone call and wherever you are be aware of the quickest way out.

TASK

Use the information given in 'Ten teenage safety tips' and make your own suggestions to give advice to teenagers who find themselves in the following situations.

a) Kate and Susan have attended a pop concert. It ended at 11 p.m. It is now 11.45 p.m. and they are waiting outside the concert hall for their prearranged lift to arrive. Their lift is forty-five minutes late. What should Kate and Susan do?

(3 marks)

b) Richard, aged fourteen, is walking home from school alone. A stranger stops his car beside him and offers Richard a lift. What should he do?

(2 marks)

c) Lucy plans to attend a weekend-long rock festival sixty miles from home. What steps should she take to ensure as safe a trip as possible?

(6 marks)

d) Debbie, aged fifteen, would like to earn some extra pocket money. What type of jobs could she do and how should she go about finding one.

(5 marks)

e) Stephen is invited to a friend's birthday party at the Beechgrove Hotel on Saturday night from 8 p.m. until midnight. Write out the conversation he has with the taxi company's receptionist when he rings to make bookings for the evening. Include the information Stephen should give and the arrangements he makes.

(9 marks)

(Total 30 marks)

Answers

Answers to Nouns and Adjectives (page 4)

1. man, house = nouns
   kind, old, dreary = adjectives

2. train, track = nouns
   fast, twisting = adjectives

3. friends, people, neighbourhood = nouns
   school, new = adjectives

4. boy, street = nouns
   young, dark = adjectives

5. birds, tree = nouns
   baby, old = adjectives

6. mother, sandwiches, picnic = nouns
   delicious = adjective

7. boy, exams = nouns
   clever, difficult = adjectives

8. France, sky, sight, holiday-makers, plane = nouns
   clear, blue, welcome = adjectives

9. road, cottage = nouns
   dusty, small, white = adjectives

10. children, park, swings = nouns
    excited, colourful = adjectives

Answers to Verbs and Adverbs (page 5)

1. yawned = verb
   lazily = adverb

2. rumbled = verb
   noisily = adverb

3. shouted = verb
   angrily = adverb

4. snored = verb
   loudly = adverb

5. rose = verb
   steadily = adverb

6. returned = verb
   warily = adverb

7. laughed, thought = verbs
   happily = adverb

8. worked = verb
   busily = adverb

9. eyed, answered = verbs
   suspiciously, cautiously = adverbs

10. encouraged = verb
    enthusiastically = adverb

Answers to Capital Letters (pages 5–6)

1. It rained last Tuesday when we went to the football match.

2. We are going on holiday in June to Spain.

3. Mary Bell is starting our school in September.

4. My mother always says that she would prefer BBC to ITV.

5. The river Seine runs through Paris.

6. My favourite book is *The Growing Pains of Adrian Mole* by Sue Townsend.

7. The girl screamed in a loud voice, "Help, get me out of here."

8. My favourite time of the year is Christmas.

9. The BBC presented *Middlemarch* by George Eliot on television during last winter.

10. Everyone hates Mondays but loves Fridays.

Answers to Full Stops and Commas (pages 6–7)

1. He ran all the way to the bus stop but the bus pulled away just as he arrived.

2. Prof. Knox was the expert on World War I.

3. Mary lived at 41 Appletree Road.

4. My favourite author is P.P. Barnes.

5. The star of the show is a tall girl with long, dark hair.

6. The pop star, who was visiting the nearby town, is my favourite singer.

7. I hate spinach, sprouts, turnips and beetroot.

8. Happily, the boy received his new birthday present.

9. The teacher stormed into the classroom, threw down the books, marched down through the rows of desks and demanded that the student should stand up.

10. Frequently, I go to the village, which is a pretty little place, to buy groceries such as butter, milk, tea and sugar.

Answers to Sentences (page 8)

1. S
3. S
5. S
6. S
7. S
10. S

Suggested Answers to Paragraphs (page 8)

1. Paragraph 1 begins 'Michael was looking forward'

2. Paragraph 2 begins 'The day of departure'

3. Paragraph 3 begins 'On arrival in Spain'

Answers to *The Mile* by George Layton (page 10)

"I'm sorry, Mum . . ."
She picked up the report again, and started reading it for the fourth time.
"It's no good reading it again, Mum. It's not going to get any better."
She slammed the report back on the table.
"Don't you make cheeky remarks to me. I'm not in the mood for it!"
I hadn't meant it to be cheeky, but I suppose it came out like that.
"I wouldn't say anything if I was you, after reading this report!"
I shrugged my shoulders.
"There's nothing much I can say, is there?"

"You can tell me what went wrong. You told me you worked hard this term!"
I had told her I'd worked hard, but I hadn't.
"I did work hard, Mum."
"Not according to this."
She waved the report under my nose.
"You're supposed to be taking your O Levels next year. What do you think is going to happen then?"
I shrugged my shoulders again, and stared at my gammon and chips.
"I don't know."

Answers to extract from *Boy* by Roald Dahl (pages 10–11)

Thus everything was arranged. We were strutting a little as we entered the shop. We were the victors now and Mrs Pratchett was the victim. She stood behind the counter, and her small malignant pig-eyes watched us suspiciously as we came forward.

"One Sherbert Sucker, please," Thwaites said to her, holding out his penny.

I kept to the rear of the group, and when I saw Mrs Pratchett turn her head away for a couple of seconds to fish a Sherbert Sucker out of the box, I lifted the heavy glass lid of the Gobstopper jar and dropped the mouse in. Then I replaced the lid as silently as possible. My heart was thumping like mad and my hands had gone all sweaty.

"And one Bootlace, please," I heard Thwaites saying. When I turned round, I saw Mrs Pratchett holding out the Bootlace in her filthy fingers.

"I don't want all the lot of you troopin' in 'ere if only one of you is buyin'," she screamed at us. "Now beat it! Go on, get out!"

As soon as we were outside, we broke into a run. "Did you do it?" they shouted at me.

"Of course I did!" I said.

"Well done you!" they cried. "What a super show!"

I felt like a hero. I *was* a hero. It was marvellous to be so popular.

Answers to Apostrophe (1) Ownership (pages 11–12)

1. Catherine's
2. the football team's
3. the workman's tools
4. the workmen's tools
5. people's health
6. teachers' meeting
7. The workers' canteen
8. a wasps' nest
9. grandfather's farm
10. Mr Smith's car

Answers to Apostrophe (2) Contraction (page 12–13)

1. does not — doesn't
2. it is — it's
3. there will — there'll
4. could not — couldn't
5. who would — who'd
6. might not — mightn't
7. I am — I'm
8. they are — they're
9. we had — we'd
10. what is — what's

Answers to Confusing Words (pages 13–14)

1. there
2. were
3. where
4. were, their, their
5. where, were

Answers to Abbreviation (pages 14–15)

1

1. On Her Majesty's Service
2. Please Turn Over
3 Member of Parliament
4. Cash on Delivery
5. Répondez s'il vous plaît (reply if you please)
6. Volkswagen
7. Rest in Peace
8. Anno Domini (Latin for 'in the year of our Lord')
9. Absent Without Leave
10. His/Her Royal Highness

5. maximum
6. Reverend
7. centimetre
8. senior
9. square
10. minute (or minimum)
11. etcetera
12. post script
13. for example
14. that is to say
15. note well

2

1. Doctor
2. street or saint
3. Saturday
4. department

3

Flat to Let
Self-contained apartment near Saint Mary's Hospital.
Sleeps four. Lounge, fitted kitchen, two double bedrooms, bathroom.
Central heating. Phone. Small garden. £150 per month.
Telephone 284691 between 6 and 9 in the evening.

Answers to Words From Other Languages (pages 16–17)

1

1. N trousers made from thick strong cloth
2. T somewhere to shelter from the snow
3. M a stupid person
4. Z to execute someone without a proper trial
5. J a frothy creamy substance
6. S a ball point pen
7. Q a dried paste made from flour and cut into shapes
8. R a fly which bites
9. U a quick cup of coffee
10. L moving quickly over snow
11. O a place where babies and young children are looked after
12. W hot and steamy place
13. X school for little children

14. Y using letters instead of numbers
15. V a house with only one storey
16. E made from sour milk
17. P tomato sauce
18. B a killer
19. C cocoa flavoured substance
20. H seizure of means of transport
21. A recording on tape
22. F an exact copy
23. I an alcoholic beverage
24. D spying
25. G to annoy
26. K to do something alone

2

1. Italian
2. Latin
3. Greek
4. Latin
5. Italian
6. Hebrew

Suggested Answers to *The Sea* by James Reeves (page 18)

1. The sea is being compared with a dog. (3 marks)

2. three adjectives   'hungry'   (1 mark)
      'giant'   (1 mark)
      'grey'   (1 mark)
These adjectives are good descriptions because they present the movement size or vastness of the sea. (3 marks)
       (total 6 marks)

3. Verse 1
 - this is a picture of the sea in day time
 - it is noisy
 - it is always moving
 - the lapping of the waves is described ('licking his greasy paws')
   (5 marks to be awarded on an impression basis)

Verse 2
 - this is a picture of the sea at night
 - it is very stormy and rough ('shaking his wet sides over the cliffs')
 - the waves are crashing and very noisy
   (5 marks to be awarded on an impression basis)

Verse 3
 - this is a picture of the sea in the summer
 - the sea is calm and peaceful
 - there is hardly a ripple on the water
   (5 marks to be awarded on an impression basis)
       (15 marks)

4. Onomatopoeic words: 'clashing', 'gnaws', 'rumbling', 'tumbling', 'moans', 'roars', 'snuffs', 'sniffs', 'howls', 'hollos', 'snores'
   (1 mark each – up to 6 marks)

Reasons why they are appropriate: these words create the idea that the sea is always noisy and never absolutely quiet. The volume of the noise depends upon the time of the year, the time of the day and weather conditions.
       (4 marks)

5. The student must give his/her own response. Marks should be awarded either way, but the student must support his/her viewpoint.
       (6 marks)
       (Total 40 marks)

Answers to *Timothy Winters* by Charles Causley (pages 19–20)

1

Similes	Effect
eyes as wide as a football-pool	Timothy's eyes were large and round
Ears like bombs	large ears which stuck out
teeth like splinters	sharp, pointed teeth, not well cared for
the law's as tricky as a ten-foot snake	to emphasise the difficulty of dealing with law. It's full of twists and turns and you get tangled up in it

2

Metaphors	Effect
A blitz of a boy	Timothy is very untidy and looks as if a bomb had just hit him
his hair is an exclamation mark	Timothy's hair sticks straight up on end
he shoots down dead the arithmetic bird	Timothy doesn't pay any attention to maths in class
He licks the patterns off his plate	Timothy scrapes every scrap of food off his plate – emphasises his hunger
Timothy Winters drinks his cup	Timothy experiences life

3

Timothy Winters is very untidy looking. He has large round eyes, ears which stick out and sharp pointed teeth. Timothy's neck is dirty and his hair sticks straight up. He is poorly dressed and his clothes are full of holes.

All these details give the impression that Timothy is not very well cared for.

4

The Welfare Worker lies awake at night worrying about Timothy and how best to help him. His father drinks, his mother has run off and Timothy is left alone with his grandmother who doses him with aspirin to make him sleep so that she can enjoy her gin in peace and quiet. The Welfare Worker can't do anything because no laws are actually being broken.

5

At morning prayers in school the master prays for less fortunate children. Timothy Winters, not realising that he is one of the less fortunate ones himself, says Amen very loudly. In the last verse the poet asks God to remember Timothy Winters and to do something to help him.

6

1. simile
2. metaphor
3. metaphor
4. metaphor
5. simile
6. simile
7. metaphor
8. simile
9. simile
10. metaphor

Suggested Mark Scheme – Empathetic Writing *Mid-Term Break* by Seamus Heaney (page 24)

Paragraph 1 – at school – how the news was broken; thoughts as he sat in the sick bay and on the journey home; perhaps some conversation might take place.

Paragraph 2 – meeting with his father; reaction to Big Jim Evans and the old men; reference to the normality of the baby; his embarrassment; the scene inside the house; holding his mother's hand; the whispers in the background.

Paragraph 3 – the arrival of the corpse; the description of the scene and his feelings at the time.

Paragraph 4 – At his brother's bedside; feelings of sorrow and anguish as he looks at the four year old.

Conclusion – the knowledge that he will never forget this child who has died.

Band 1 response Factual response reporting what happened, written fairly accurately. Perhaps some general feelings conveyed.

(1–10 marks)

Band 2 response Accurate account of what happened; attempt to identify with the boy's feelings at the different stages of the poem.

(11–20 marks)

Band 3 response Clear identification with the boy and the experience he is going through. There should be detailed reference to what is happening in the poem and afterwards.

(21–30 marks)

(Total 30 marks)

Suggested Answers to extract from *Taming of the Shrew* by William Shakespeare (page 26–27)

Such points could be made in the article:

- headline should be short conveying the strangeness of the wedding, for example 'Grumbling groom and devil wed'.

- both groom and bride shout at one another.

- bridegroom swears.

- priest drops his prayer book.

- bridegroom hits the priest.

- priest falls.

- bridegroom stamps his feet.

- the bride trembles and shakes.

- bridegroom calls for wine in the middle of the ceremony as if he were out with his mates, throwing the dregs from the cup at the churchwarden.

- bridegroom kisses bride in such a loud way that the church echoes.

- it is a 'mad marriage'.

- they return after the wedding singing and dancing.

Suggested Answer and Mark Scheme to Letters (Business or Formal) (pages 27–28)

The layout should be as follows.

23 Marlborough Park,
Lisburn Road,
Cardiff,
CF42 4OP.

26 February 1995

Mr K. Park,
UK Sleep Support Group,
450 Aberdare Enterprise Centre,
Aberaman Industrial Park,
Mid Glamorgan,
CF44 6DA.

Dear Mr Park,

I wish to reply to your letter which appeared in the *Belfast Telegraph* of 10 February 1994. I was very interested to read about the help and support you are supplying for people who have difficulty sleeping.

My aunt has a severe problem getting to sleep. Sometimes it can take her three hours to fall asleep. She has tried everything: having a hot drink before she goes to bed; reading to help her relax; even going to bed later. None of these things seem to work. She just ends up exhausted the next day.

I would really like to help my aunt with her difficulties and think that your information pack might be the first step to the solution of her problems. I should be very grateful if you would send your information pack to the above address. I enclose two stamps as requested.

Yours sincerely,

Jenny Smith

Jenny Smith

Layout: Own address address and date in top right hand corner.
(5 marks)

Name and address of recipient on left hand side of page.
(5 marks)

Correct opening and conclusion.
(5 marks)

Content: Paragraph 1 – reason for writing letter is stated clearly/where and when the letter appeared is stated.
(5 marks)

Paragraph 2 – an appropriate account of why help is required is outlined.
(5 marks)

Paragraph 3 – request for information pack is made.
(5 marks)

Tone: The request for an information pack is made politely. The tone of the letter is formal.
(10 marks)

(Total 40 marks)

Suggested Mark Scheme for Letter of Complaint to a flower company (page 29)

Layout: Own address and date in top right hand corner.
(5 marks)

Name and address of company on the left hand side of page.
(5 marks)

Correct opening and conclusion.
(5 marks)

Content: Paragraph 1 – reference to the details of the order you placed with the company.
(5 marks)

Paragraph 2 – nature of the complaint.
(5 marks)

Paragraph 3 – polite request for a full refund. (5 marks)

Tone: The case for a refund should be explained firmly but politely. The tone of the letter should be formal.
(10 marks)

(Total 40 marks)

Suggested Answers to Newspaper Article on Noise (page 30)

These are the points which should be included in the article.

Layout:
1. Headline should be eye-catching.

2. Alliteration or humour may feature.

3. Paragraphs must be used, and ability to connect ideas should be rewarded.
(Layout 10 marks)

Content:
4. The main facts should be given.
(5 marks)

5. Interviews with people affected by noise should be rewarded.
(5 marks)

6. Evidence of personal research should be rewarded.
(5 marks)
(Content 15 marks)

(Total 25 marks)

Suggested Answer to Making a Complaint (pages 31–32)

It is important that the tone of the conversation is polite.

MANAGER: Good morning, Madam. Can I help you?

CUSTOMER: Good morning. Thank you very much. I would like to speak to the manager (or person in charge).

MANAGER: I'm the person in charge of the ladies' shoe department. How can I help?

CUSTOMER: I'd be very grateful if you'd look at these shoes. I've only worn them a few times and the heel has come off them. I bought them here a couple of weeks ago. I would like them replaced or a full refund.

MANAGER: Do you have your receipt?

CUSTOMER: No, I'm very sorry I don't. I remember that the assistant who served me had blonde hair, but as this is a very busy store which must sell a large number of shoes it is unlikely that she would remember me.

MANAGER: I understand. However, without a receipt I can't refund your money, but I am prepared to offer you a replacement pair of shoes. I can see that the shoes have not been worn much and we do sell that particular make. Would you be prepared to accept that?

CUSTOMER: Yes. Thank you very much for your time and your help. I'll certainly come back here when I need another pair of shoes.

Suggested Answers for 'Playing for your life' (page 36)

Kids of the 1990s are increasingly likely to develop heart problems, unless they take more exercise. (1 mark)

Report by Dr Colin Boreham QUB. (2 marks)

Only 10 per cent walk or cycle to school. (2 marks)

Health problems will develop at an earlier age. (1 mark)

Video, TV and computers mostly to blame. (3 marks)

Parents also reluctant to allow their children to play unsupervised. (1 mark)

Adventure playgrounds – a possible solution; safe, vigorous play under supervision. For example, Gulliver's Kingdom which holds up to 250 children and has a range of physical activities. (5 marks)

(Total 15 marks)

Suggested Answers to *Three Lambs* by Liam O'Flaherty (page 37)

1. He was going to watch the black sheep having a lamb. (2 marks)

2. • drinks cold milk even though he hates it.
   • lifted the latch gently and stole out.
   • was in a great hurry and tears his jersey.
   • gets up before dawn.
   • thought the lane would never end.
   • takes off his shoes and stockings to cover the ground faster.

   2 marks each for any of the above points or any phrases which indicate excitement. (up to 10 marks)

3. Little Michael's family has more money than Little Jimmy's family.
   Little Michael wears shoes and stockings during part of the year but Little Jimmy doesn't.

Little Michael is the son of a magistrate and Little Jimmy is the son of a farm labourer.
Little Jimmy is admired by all the little boys in the school rather than Little Michael.

2 marks for each of these four reasons. (up to 8 marks)

4. This question should be marked on general impression but the following points should be used as a guide:
   Little Michael's excitement and urgency to get to the sheep in time should be presented.
   The difficulty of the journey should be described, for example travelling across fields, uneven ground, etc.
   The thrill when he finds the sheep should be described.
   His reaction to the lamb's birth and how he cares for the sheep should be included. (up to 20 marks)

(Total 40 marks)

Suggested Answers to *Mid-Term Break* by Seamus Heaney (pages 38–39)

1. The poet has come home from boarding school / for the funeral of his four year old brother / who has been killed in a car accident. (3 marks)

2. A mid-term break is usually looked forward to as a break from lessons and hard work./ This particular break from school is different / the boy has to go home because his younger brother is dead. (3 marks)

3. Bells in school usually are described as ringing, / a funeral bell knells / The effect of this word is to introduce the idea of death to the reader, / even before he knows what has happened. (4 marks)

4. His father's reaction was surprising because he has always 'taken funerals in his stride' / In other words he had not shown that he was upset by them and had always been able to cope. / On this occasion, however, he was crying and was very obviously distressed. (3 marks)

5. The baby was the only person acting normally / because he was too young to understand what had happened. (2 marks)

6. He was embarrassed because these men, much older than himself, were treating him as an equal (grown-up) / when they stood up to shake his hand and offer him sympathy. (2 marks)

7. The two phrases used are 'it was a hard blow' and 'sorry for my trouble'. / The poet has chosen them to reflect the type of speech actually used on such occasions/euphemisms for death. (3 marks)

8. Whereas the father cried, the mother did not cry./ She was angry / and sighed, and she held the boy's hand. (3 marks)

9. The young child had died in a car accident, but now all is calm and quiet ./ There are bunches of snowdrops beside the bed / and the room is lit by candles./ The colour white,

(innocence and purity) and the light from the candle symbolising life after death prevail, and all is peaceful.

(4 marks)

10. The use of the word poppy conveys the redness of the bruise, / but also suggests remembrance. / The poppy is the symbol of remembrance and the poet is suggesting here that he will never forget his brother.

(3 marks)

11. The effect of the last line is to shock / it stands as a verse on its own / the reader is told in an indirect way that the child who died was only four years old / alliteration is used / to enhance the rhythm / the line consists of two clearly separated statements. The abrupt sudden ending reflects the abrupt sudden ending of a young life.

(6 marks)

12. Accept valid reasons which give evidence of a personal response.

(4 marks)

(Total 40 marks)

Suggested Answers to *Warning* by Jenny Joseph (page 39)

1. a) First verse she states she will 'make up for the sobriety of my youth' which suggests she resents having had such a sensible early youth and now need no longer conform.

(2 marks)

b) In the second verse she suggests that she is looking forward to doing things as and when she wants to do them.

(2 marks)

c) The third verse opens by saying 'But now . . .' indicating an annoyance at having to accept things as they are in the present. She then suggests that she should begin practising her new lifestyle.

(2 marks)

2. She will: a) wear purple clothes and a hat that doesn't match or suit her
b) spend money on brandy and luxury items
c) pretend she hasn't money for basics
d) sit down wherever she happens to be
e) eat food samples in shops
f) press alarm bells and create a noise
g) wear slippers outside
h) pick flowers in other people's gardens
i) spit
j) grow fat, not having to think about what she's eating
k) store things away

(10 marks)

3. She has to behave sensibly, giving a good example to the children.

(1 mark)

4. To indicate to others that she might behave like this – to prepare them for a dramatic change in her appearance and behaviour.

(3 marks)

5. a) Headline should be eye-catching – short, perhaps alliteration.

b) Writer has free range to present this character in a favourable or unfavourable way but should indicate the eccentricity of the character.

(10 marks)

(Total 30 marks)

Suggested Answers to 'Seven Ages of Man' by William Shakespeare (page 40)

1. a) The baby (is crying and being sick).
b) The schoolboy (going to school very reluctantly).
c) The young person (romantic and in love).
d) The soldier (the young man full of determination and impetuosity).
e) The judge/lawyer (age of sense and wisdom).
f) Old person (getting foolish).
g) Very old person – ('senile dementia').

(14 marks)

2. Stage represents the whole world with people interacting with others at different stages of their lives. Each of the seven phases represents a different act in the play of life. (6 marks)

3. One of these:

'creeping like snail' – crawling reluctantly – a snail moves very slowly.

'sighing like furnace' – like bellows blowing air into a furnace to make the fire hotter.

'bearded like a pard' – a leopard has short, dense hair
– the soldier has a first growth of beard.

(10 marks)

4. Man – mind wandering
no teeth/gaps
eyesight is poor

(6 marks)

5. An imaginative response is expected showing awareness of the feelings and attitudes of the individual described.

(14 marks)

(Total 50 marks)

ANSWERS

Suggested Answers to extract from *Shadows on the Lake* by Catherine Sefton (pages 40–42)

1. a) Baxter has been involved in something dangerous.
b) Baxter can be trusted.
c) Allie likes him and believed in him.
d) Allie didn't 'fancy' him.
e) Annie had thought he was a thief.
f) Perhaps Annie 'used' him.
g) Baxter is Annie's brother.
h) He is selfless, does things to help others, not for himself.
(8 marks)

2. a) Annie is annoyed at Allie.
b) Annie is determined to say exactly what she thinks to Allie.
c) Allie trusted Baxter, she recognised his qualities.
d) Allie liked him but didn't 'fancy' Baxter.
e) Allie was being watched by the police.
f) Allie has protected her father and saved him from being killed.
g) She admits to using Baxter.
h) Gets angry with Annie and forces her to realise the importance of trusting others. (8 marks)

3. a) Recognises that Allie was right to protect her father.
b) Allie wasn't mean but loved her father just as Annie loves hers.
c) She had spent too long not trusting people, feeling the whole world was against her because her mother had been taken away from her.
d) She recognises that her Dad had reasons for not telling her about her mother's illness.
e) They were going to change their lifestyle, no more moping around and they were going to look after one another.
f) They shouldn't bottle things up but allow a new trust to develop between them. (6 marks)

4. Your diary should:
• be written in first person.
• reflect on what Annie thought about Allie and how she has changed her view.
• Annie's love for her Dad.
• how Annie must trust people.
• how Annie must build for the future.
• refer to actual incidents which have taken place and will take place the next day. (18 marks)

(Total 40 marks)

Suggested Mark scheme for *No Good Crying Now* (pages 42–43)

1. The mother thought the child had been knocked over. (1 mark)

2. To get the doll mended. (1 mark)

3. Any four of the following points:
• given to child by her father
• called Jean
• made from special china
• had very large head
• unusual doll
• used to model babies' clothes (4 marks)

4. Peckham (1 mark)

5. She felt the sting (½ mark)
There was an imprint on her leg for hours (½ mark)

6. It was a precious doll given to her by her father when she was a toddler.
She had been repeatedly warned not to take her into the street.
The girl was supposed to play with her doll in the front room where there was carpet so that if she should drop her she wouldn't break. (3 marks)

7. He had bright thick auburn hair despite his age.
He had one blue eye, one brown, and a high pitched voice. (2 marks)

8. Her head was not average size, and was made of special china. (2 marks)

9. The following points to be included:
• seemed a real person to the child, not a doll
• could tell doll all her secrets and feelings
• shared her likes and dislikes
• her special friend (5 marks)

10. straight narrative account of story (1–4 marks)

narrative but including feelings of girl at the time of the incident (5–7 marks)

clear empathy with character, covering range of her feelings then, and now as she is looking back (8–10 marks)

(Total 30 marks)

A12

Suggested Mark Scheme for The *Early Purges* by Seamus Heaney (pages 44–45)

1. pitched into a bucket
   water pumped in
   left to drown   (3 marks)

2. scraggy wee shits
   a frail metal sound
   soft paws
   tiny din   (4 marks)

3. wet gloves
   simile   (2 marks)

4. he was frightened and hung around
   the dung-heap watching them decay   (2 marks)

5. drowned the kittens
   pulled old hens' necks – thought he was being cruel to be
   kind 'Sure isn't it better for them now'
   trapped rats, snared rabbits, shot crows, kept pests down,
   drowned pups, was not sentimental about animals   (7 marks)

6. upset when he was young, now accepts it as a necessity on a
   farm. 'I just shrug. Bloody pups. It makes sense'. (3 marks)

7. Say it is cruelty and should be prevented. In towns the death
   of animals is considered unnatural but 'on well-run farms
   pests have to be kept down'.   (4 marks)

8. Credit valid personal response to the poem.   (5 marks)
   All aspects of the question should be attempted.

   (Total 30 marks)

Suggested Answers to extract from *Hard Times* by Charles Dickens (page 45)

1. He worked in a bank. He was involved in buying and selling
   things. He was involved in the production of goods. (4 marks)

2. Bounderby seems to be involved in every type of occupation –
   he is banker, merchant and manufacturer. It seems that
   Dickens is saying that Bounderby has experience of
   everything; anything would be within his capabilities. It could
   also be suggested that Dickens is mocking him and
   wondering how anyone could have all these occupations.
                                                       (3 marks)

3. He is very large in size and has wide, pronounced, staring
   eyes. He has a very loud voice and when he laughs his laugh
   is so loud it echoes and reverberates.   (5 marks)

4. He is so fat he seems to be almost circular. It could also
   suggest that he is inflated in the sense that he thinks that he
   is so important or 'full of himself'. It seems that he is so large
   (like a balloon) that if you put a pin to him he would burst.
                                                       (3 marks)

5. He is proud of how he has changed – how someone who
   started with nothing has ended up being very important.
                                                       (3 marks)

6. No.
   He is boastful 'who could never sufficiently vaunt himself a
   self-made man'.
   He is horrible to look at 'a great puffed head and forehead'
   'made out of coarse material'.
   Conceited, proud, enjoys saying what a great person he is.
   Bullies ordinary people by showing off his skills.
                                                (max for q. 6, 7 marks)

   (Total 25 marks)

Suggested Answers to 'Make Mother's Day' (pages 46–47)

1. The customer is being offered a choice of three luxury bouquets of carnations delivered in time for Mother's Day.
(2 marks)

2. This advertisement is being aimed at adults with mothers to whom they wish to send flowers. (3 marks)

3. The cheapest bouquet is £8.99. (1 mark)

4. Bouquet No.1 at £11.99 contains 10 long stem and 5 spray carnations while the second contains 10 long stem carnations. (2 marks)

5. Included in the price of each order are fern, flower food and a personal message. (3 marks)

6. Each bouquet is packaged in a sturdy designer gift box.
(1 mark)

7. The two methods by which you can place your order are by phone and by post. (2 marks)

8. The flowers can be paid for by cheque, postal order or credit card. (3 marks)

9. The closing date for the order is March 4th. (1 mark)

10. If you wish to place an additional order you must, on a separate piece of paper / write the name and address of the person to whom the bouquet is to be sent / your name and address / and the message to be included with the flowers.
(4 marks)

11. No. You do not have to pay extra for postage. The word 'inclusive' tells you this. (2 marks)

12. The words and phrases in this advertisement which imply this is an offer not to be missed are: 'Make Mother's Day', 'luxury longstem carnations', '1st class post', 'only £8.99', 'included in the price are . . .', 'presented in a sturdy designer gift box', 'delivered to her door from Jersey', 'two other great value for money offers', 'luxury carnations' (repeated), 'incredibly low prices'.
(any 6 – up to a maximum of 6 marks)

(Total 30 marks)

Suggested Answers to RSPB extract (pages 48–50)

1. Leighton Moss is near Silverdale, just off the A6 at Carnforth.
(1 mark for each point)
(total 3 marks)

2. Call 01283 51011 (1 mark)
Monday–Friday (1 mark)
9.00am–5.00pm (1 mark)
payment by credit card (1 mark)
or switch card (1 mark)
(total 5 marks)

3. K   Butterfly Garden   61-58-70   at £8.50
(1 mark for each point)
(total 4 marks)

4. 14–28 days (2 marks)

5. elusive = difficult to catch (2 marks)
embossed motif = main symbol which stands out (4 marks)
durable = long lasting (2 marks)
perennials = plants living several years (2 marks)
denotes = indicates (2 marks)

6. Any combination of items would be suitable provided appropriate reasons are given and approximately £20 is spent. (8 marks)

7. Allow for answers arguing either way provided the answer is supported. (6 marks)

(Total 40 marks)

Suggested Answers to Advertisement Questionnaire (pages 52–53)

1. a) Junior mouth guard (1 mark)
   b) Macleans (1 mark)

2. (most likely). The pictures of the bottle of mouth guard, the dentist's drill (1 mark)

3. Writing in bold print at top of page contrast between black and white and coloured pictures, writing at bottom of page. (3 marks)

4. Parents of young children. (1 mark)

5. Makes them feel that they can help their children to have good teeth and avoid painful dental treatment. (1 mark)

6. Fear of not being a good parent. (2 marks)

7. **Images:**   **Language**
   grey frightening drill   new
   with sharp needle point   great taste
   colourful attractive bottle   play on words – which drill?

contrast in the two images   conversational tone of main text
large writing on the bottle label   specially formulated unbeatable protection Macleans where a kid's toothbrush can't
(any 10 points, 1 mark each)

8. The slogan (Macleans where a kid's toothbrush can't), the pictures with use of contrast, the pun on 'drill'. (3 marks)

9. It implies that this is the solution to tooth decay. (1 mark)

10. Price. (1 mark)

11. Personal opinion backed up by evidence from the advertisement. All aspects of the question should be considered. (5 marks)

(Total 30 marks)

Suggested Answers to Other Ways of Presenting Information (pages 54–55)

The European Union

1. a) Brussels – European Parliament Committees
   b) Luxembourg – European Parliament Staff and Offices
   c) Strasbourg – European Parliament main chamber (6 marks)

2. Largest – Germany 81 million
   Smallest – Luxembourg 400,000 (2 marks)

3. 567 MEPs in 1994 (1 mark)

4. Germany has eighteen extra seats, to accommodate the union of West and East Germany. (2 marks)

5. Belgium has 7.8 million voters. (1 mark)

6. Italy, Portugal, Spain, Greece, Germany, Netherlands, UK, France, Belgium. (9 marks)

7. Socialist group. (1 mark)

8. If they are anti-EC it is an irony that they should hold seats in its Parliament. (1 mark)

9. Paragraph 1 – the countries, their names, the number of voters, their population size.

   – perhaps some comment on which countries wield most power to gain high marks in this section. (5 marks)

   Paragraph 2 – the parties – comment should be made on the wide variety of parties represented. (5 marks)

   Paragraph 3 – valid personal opinions should be credited (5 marks)

10. a)

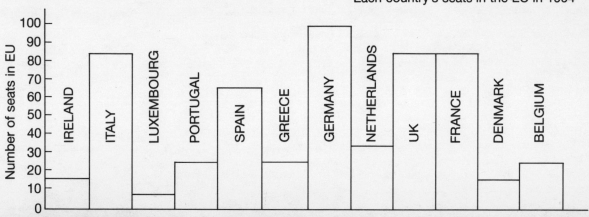

Each country's seats in the EU in 1994

10. b)

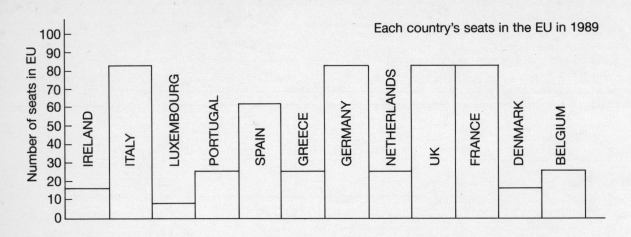

Each country's seats in the EU in 1989

10. c) Benefits: clarity
information is easier to understand   (12 marks)

(Total 50 marks)

Ten teenage safety tips

a)   – speak to the organisers
– use their telephone to make arrangements
– ask to stay until transport arrives   (3 marks)

b) – refuse politely
   – move on quickly   (2 marks)

c) Lucy should:
   – make sure her parents know where she is and how to contact her, and when to expect her back.
   – go accompanied by friends and return with them.
   – make all transport arrangements beforehand for both journey there and back.
   – refuse to accept lifts either from complete strangers or people she has just met.
   – be aware of how to make an emergency call or how to reverse the charges.
   – make sure she has sufficient money with her.   (6 marks)

d) babysitting   paper round   (2 marks)

Debbie should:
   – try to find a job through family and friends.
   – be careful about answering advertisements.
   – try to go with a parent or a friend on the first day. (3 marks)

e) Stephen's conversation with the receptionist must include the following points:
   • date and time of journey to the hotel.
   • address where he should be picked up.
   • names of destination.
   • date and time of return journey.
   • confirmation of name of hotel.
   • estimate of cost.
   • payment for two single journeys or for round trip.
   • details of who to contact in the event of the taxi not turning up.
   • is it necessary to confirm the booking nearer to the time?
            (9 marks)

(Total 25 marks)